The Politics of Time and
Youth in Brand India

DIVERSITY AND PLURALITY IN SOUTH ASIA

The *Diversity and Plurality in South Asia* series, wide in
scope, will bring together publications in anthropology and
sociology, alongside politics and international relations, exploring
themes of both contemporary and historical relevance. This diverse line
in the social sciences and humanities will investigate the plurality of
social groups, identities and ideologies, including within its remit
not only interrogations of issues surrounding gender, caste,
religion and region, but also political variations, and a
variety of cultural ideas and expressions
within South Asia.

Series Editor

Nandini Gooptu – University of Oxford, UK

ANTHEM GLOBAL MEDIA AND COMMUNICATION STUDIES

Anthem Global Media and Communication Studies aims to
advance the understandings of the continuously changing global
media and communication environment. The series publishes critical
scholarly studies and high-quality edited volumes on key issues and debates
in the field (as well as the occasional trade book and the more practical
'how-to' guide) on all aspects of media, culture and communication studies.
We invite work that examines not only recent phenomena in this field but
also at studies which theorize the continuities between different technologies,
topics, eras and methodologies. Saliently, building on the interdisciplinary
strengths of this field, we particularly welcome cutting edge research
in and at the intersection of communication and media studies,
anthropology, cultural studies, sociology, telecommunications,
public policy, migration and diasporic studies, gender studies,
transnational politics and international relations.

Series Editors

Shakuntala Banaji – London School of Economics and
Political Science (LSE), UK
Terhi Rantanen – London School of Economics and
Political Science (LSE), UK

The Politics of Time and Youth in Brand India

Bargaining with Capital

Jyotsna Kapur

ANTHEM PRESS
LONDON · NEW YORK · DELHI

Anthem Press
An imprint of Wimbledon Publishing Company
www.anthempress.com

This edition first published in UK and USA 2014
by ANTHEM PRESS
75–76 Blackfriars Road, London SE1 8HA, UK
or PO Box 9779, London SW19 7ZG, UK
and
244 Madison Ave #116, New York, NY 10016, USA

First published in hardback by Anthem Press in 2013

British Library Cataloguing-in-Publication Data
A catalogue record for this book is available from the British Library.

Library of Congress Cataloging-in-Publication Data
The Library of Congress has catalogued the hardcover edition as follows:
Kapur, Jyotsna.
The politics of time and youth in brand India : bargaining with
capital / Jyotsna Kapur.
pages cm
Includes bibliographical references and index.
ISBN 978-0-85728-109-8 (hardcover : alk. paper) – ISBN
0-85728-109-7 (hardcover : alk. paper)
1. India–Social conditions–21st century. 2. Youth–India. 3.
Branding (Marketing)–India. 4. Neoliberalism–India. I. Title.
HC435.3.K363 2013
306.30954–dc23
2013032093

ISBN-13: 978 1 78308 353 4 (Pbk)
ISBN-10: 1 78308 353 0 (Pbk)

Cover photo © Mike Covell 2010

This title is also available as an ebook.

For time flows on, and if it did not it would be a poor look-out for those who have no golden tables to sit at. Methods wear out, stimuli fail. New problems loom up and demand new techniques. Reality alters; to represent it the means of representation must alter too. Nothing arises from nothing; the new springs from the old, but that is just what makes it new.

—Bertolt Brecht

If we are unable to build, and build in time, a socialist alternative worthy of the name, what capitalism now promises us is only a future of barbarism. And since the possibility of the destruction of our world itself cannot be ruled out, it could well be a future of no future at all. [...] Yet, nothing is inevitable in human affairs until it happens. In the final analysis it is how we struggle and fight back that will decide our future. We can still make our future our own way, build it as a society of freedom and equality and a truly rich human life for us all – for that is what socialism is about.

—Randhir Singh

[...] the world has long since dreamed of something of which it needs only to become conscious for it to possess it in reality. [...] our task is not to draw a sharp mental line between past and future, but to complete the thought of the past. [...] mankind will not begin any new work, but will consciously bring about the completion of its old work.

—Karl Marx

Why fear, if in our desire for dawn we too are swallowed whole by this dark night? There will be some people, at least, who will live to see the bright morning.

—Jagmohan Joshi

CONTENTS

ACKNOWLEDGMENTS

This book has been a long time in the making and many people have shared in its journey. I wish to thank Beryl Langer, Sue Ferguson, Alan Sears, Elizabeth Chin, Robbie Lieberman, Robin Andersen, Toby Miller, Aarti Wani, Nandini Chandra, Samina Misra, Keith Wagner, Deborah Tudor and Eileen Meehan for their critical engagement and help in shaping this project. I must also thank my students for listening, challenging, and putting up with what must have appeared to be an obsession with space, time, cinema and capitalism. Their generosity remained undiminished in these days of imposed austerity from the top. Finally, my union, the SIUC Faculty Association, provided perspective, humor and a place to understand and challenge neoliberalism and its consequences for our young people.

Then there are people with whom one goes back a long way, who have so helped shape my political and personal life that it would be impossible to isolate my own ideas from those developed with them. Professor Randhir Singh has remained my inspiration, including for this work. Even now, more than three decades since I sat in his classes on political theory at Delhi University, I draw upon the passion and clarity with which he made us see that another world was possible. Chuck Kleinhans, Vrinda Grover, Amar Kanwar, Savia Veigas, Myron Periera, O. P. Bakshi, Barry John and Sumit Sarkar and Tanika Sarkar will find themselves in these pages. It was just one long conversation with Dilip Simeon, but he made me see the centrality of the politics of time and helped bring this book to an end.

As always, Nilim and Suhaila put up, with their usual humor and patience, with a mother who frequently lost track of time. Our home rings with laughter over forgotten errands and dates, including sometimes even the children's ages. Perhaps, writing is a way to forget the invariable passing of time. I often thought of my father, an academic himself, telling my brother and me that teachers may not have a lot of money, but they had lots of time. And my parents knew how to make that time happy – filling our childhood with their comrades, laughter and adults who either spoke to us seriously or not at all. So, thank you Narinder Singh and Satinder Kapur for that very honest childhood. And thanks to Ankur, Ajinder, Depinder, Mini, Satnam, Sumi and Sanjam, who make coming home still just as delightful. Mary and Dick Schuler, despite living far away, remain a constant presence. Mike Covell shared my life and, as in everything else, helped separate the fluff from the substance. It is just as much fun being at home with him as it is on the picket line.

A Fulbright grant as well as a National Endowment for the Humanities summer stipend earned me the time to dedicate to this volume. Chapter 4 was first published in *Communication, Culture & Critique* (vol. 2, no. 2, pp. 221–33, 2009); Chapter 5 was published in *Visual Anthropology* (vol. 22, no. 2/3, p 155–66, 2009). Tye Wilson's help with reproducing the images in this book and Suhaila Meera's research assistance is much appreciated. I also wish to offer my heartfelt thanks to Tej P. S. Sood, Rob Reddick and Brian Stone at Anthem Press for their patience and encouragement. Finally, this book was vastly improved by the careful reading of the copyeditor, Meredith Ramey.

Introduction

AFTER ME THE FLOOD

It is spring. And all at once have returned from the distant past
Those dreams, the youth
That had died on your lips
And after each death been born again

[…]

It is spring. And one by one, the old accounts
All the questions and answers, yours and mine,
Have been reopened
Once again, from a new beginning.

—Faiz Ahmed Faiz[1]

Evoking the longing for revolution in words that could have been addressed to a beloved, the Marxist Urdu poet, Faiz Ahmed Faiz, inscribes revolutionary struggles with a sense of time that is at once immanent and transcendent. In other words, while specific people rebel in specific historical contexts and circumstances, they hope to transcend that history and bring in a new future. It is this time-consciousness that defeats failure, for, as Faiz reminds us, even defeat carries within it the seeds of another rebirth. Making a revolution was, for Faiz, an act of love that might end in loss (hence, dreams that have died on "your lips") and a striving for authentic life that simultaneously united "lovers" in the present and across history – so long as injustice remained intact. Faiz wrote this couplet in 1975, and I read it here as the determined recognition of a generation who, having defeated the colonial rulers, must now reckon with postcolonial "national" elites passing off their class interests as those of the nation – a nation that, by 1975, was partitioned into three countries.

In another rendering of the same theme, this time in the popular Hindi film *Rang De Basanti* (Color Me Saffron) (Mehra and D'Silva 2006), the young protagonists – facing certain death at the hands of a corrupt nexus between the state, security forces and business – indict the politicians of India for having "sold" the country. The historical context, in this case, is the Indian state's formal adoption in 1991 of the principles of neoliberalism under the supervision of the International Monetary Fund (IMF) and World Bank. In this particular film, the young remind their elders of a history the latter have chosen to forget, that is, the struggles and sacrifices of a generation that had won India its freedom from the British Empire. The film claims that to use this freedom to further private profit is a betrayal of the history and sacrifices of an earlier generation.[2]

When grandchildren stoke a memory – still alive in a generation that lived through India's first decolonization – it can unleash a heady call to action. At the very least, it sutures the fragmentation of capitalistic time in which the new incessantly erases the old. Instead, it reconciles generations, restores the power of memory, and deepens outrage with history. This book is about the profound ways in which India's turn to neoliberalism is accompanied by a heightened awareness of the politics of time and age. Neoliberalism, or the return to the principles of the free market from a century and half earlier, has intensified the impression – most certainly amongst those aware of history – that something is being undone rather than built anew with the Indian State's formal adoption of the policy of "structural adjustment" in 1991. While state and business dogma casts this shift as India's break from history, there is an intense preoccupation with the cultural politics of time itself, manifested in a preoccupation with youth and the relation between generations.

There are two concepts from Marxist theory that I will rely on to explain the nature of time and generational politics fathered by capitalism. The first is the notion of capitalist development as a systemic form of underdevelopment that perpetuates a radicalized individualism while simultaneously erasing the sense of selfhood as life appears increasingly unfree, risky and uncertain. For instance, the loss of a job – even a highly paid one in the corporate sector – drives people to suicide. At the level of everyday experience, such precarity is experienced as an ever-escalating race against time. The second concept I will draw upon is Marx's critique of the time-orientation of capitalism: its self-representation as a system of change that promises freedom while, in fact, the process of proletarianization reduces life to the barest abstraction, that is, into mere units of time to be exchanged for a wage, and thus ultimately meaningless.

Amongst the deepest contradictions set in motion by India's transition to neoliberalism, I will argue, is a heightened awareness of time and a fragmented time-consciousness in which the past, the present and the future are experienced as severed from each other. There is a widespread preoccupation with youth, novelty, and the speeding up of time as the shift to neoliberalism is presented as a break from history. For instance, advertisements marketing a

Kal bane woh aaj banega
India aaj ka aaj banega

IndiaFirst
LIFE INSURANCE

Figure 1. A billboard advertising life insurance reads: "What it would have accomplished tomorrow it will do today; India will come into its own here and today." Photo © the author, 2009.

range of products from soda to clothes advocate giving up past habits of thrift and living in the moment. Television soaps endlessly rehearse the conflict between self-invention over adhering to tradition, between living for oneself in the moment versus postponing gratification for an uncertain future. Some of the most brutal battles are being fought in the arena of sexuality. While contemporary consumer culture paints a picture of sexual freedom (albeit to be realized only through the purchase of brand names) personal autonomy has drastically diminished with widening antagonisms in society.

The dominant rhetoric justifies neoliberalism as a break from history. We are told that India has no use for history because it is in the midst of reinventing itself as a global economic power. This claim is made on the backs of a new generation that is claimed to be radically different from previous generations. Variously characterized as the "global generation," "children of liberalization" or "zippies" these under-thirty-year-olds are supposed to have shot out of India's history as a Third World country to emerge as world-class consumers.

The promise of novelty, of joining the "saga of great adventure and enterprise," as the current prime minister and the architect of India's structural adjustment policies, Manmohan Singh, describes it, is the key to naturalizing neoliberalism – for to oppose this change is to invite the fate of the dinosaur.[3] And novelty is the driving feature of the culture of capitalism. It is repeatedly asserted through the market choices and international brands that have become ubiquitous on the multiple screens of the Indian landscape, including the experience of window shopping, driving by billboards and staring at televisions or movie screens. Never mind that the actual buyers of these market commodities have to be ensconced within the privatized enclaves of malls and gated communities, their "freedom" guarded by economic barriers and outright state, paramilitary and private militia forces and maintained by the erasure of history.

While marketers and advertisers celebrate the freedom of children as consumers, parents and teachers are being told to discipline their children into a lifetime of labor in an increasingly flexible and informal economy, where employment is never guaranteed and one has to be ready to reinvent oneself along the changing demands of the workplace. It is in this environment that US president Barack Obama's remarks to US middle- and working-class parents – blaming them for the failure of young people at the job market – have turned into self-congratulatory claims about the virtues of Asian parenting in India. Obama was widely quoted in the Indian national press for the following:

> The Chinese, the Indians, they are coming at us and they're coming at us hard, and they're hungry, and they're really buckling down. Their kids watch a lot less TV than our kids do, play a lot fewer video games, they are in the classroom a lot longer. (*Indian Express* 2009)

In both tone and content, these remarks echo neoliberal advocates such as Thomas Friedman (2005) who blame US parents and young people rather than the economic recession for the failure to get jobs. At the time of this writing, the US had an official unemployment rate of 8.1 percent (United States Department of Labor 2012). It is also a not-too-subtle way to deflect working- and middle-class anger away from the bankers, the capitalists and the national elites by deploying a racist rhetoric that pits workers against each other. Ultimately, it boils down to robbing young people in both countries of childhood and youth as a time of play and self-discovery.

Marxist Theory and Anti-capitalist Time-Orientation

In this book, I will outline the contours of this new obsession with youth and time-consciousness and trace its links to capitalism, now radicalized as neoliberalism, and suggest that Marxist theory offers a critique of capitalistic time-consciousness as well as an alternative conception of time that is worthy of human life. In the "spring" of every new generation's protest, Faiz seems to say, the unredeemed longings of the past are reborn. In other words, it is the simultaneous consciousness of memory and desire or the awareness of both the past and the future that frees humans from the limitations of mortality and time. The exact opposite of such freedom is the homogenous and linear time-discipline of the clock that moves in absolute equally measured intervals where time, once lost, can never be regained. Profits are calculated, capital invested and realized, and surplus value generated against the incessant rotation of the hands of a clock, which move along homogenous intervals, incessantly and permanently dissolving the future into the present and the present into the past. In other words, when capitalists say time is money they measure time by the clock, considering every minute a lost opportunity if not used to generate profit.

Yet, as Henri Bergson noted in *Creative Evolution* and *Matter and Memory* at the beginning of the twentieth century (1911a, 15; 1911b, 75–7), human time-consciousness is more complex and multi-layered than the clicking of a clock. Bergson countered that to think of time only in terms of a clock was to reduce our perception of time to spatial terms as if we were capable of occupying (like space) only a single moment in time; a moment which would quickly recede into the past. The reduction of time into a spatial category is evidenced in the standard reply to the question: What time is it? Answer: 7 AM. According to the clock, there can only be one specific answer to this question. Yet, as Bergson understood so well, the human perception of time runs deeper than that singular, simplistic awareness of a moment. Every moment in human consciousness, Bergson explained, is imbued with memory and desire, that is, we think in duration.[4]

There is a striking illustration of time-consciousness that goes beyond clock time in Michael Moore's documentary, *Roger & Me* ([1989] 2003). It is the last day of the General Motors plant and the workers – who are now going to join the ranks of the unemployed – cheer as the last car comes through the assembly line. Moore's camera frames a worker visibly frustrated by this cheering. He looks straight into the camera and says, "Some people do not know what time it is." The time he is speaking of is not 5 PM or 4 PM or even the closing of the factory, but it is the time that has yet to come for these workers and, as the film goes on, for the labor movement as a whole. In her careful reading of Bergson, Bliss Cua Lim (2009) explains that Bergson's intellectual achievement was that he temporalized freedom, that is, he traced the possibility or desire of freedom in the human awareness of time. As she elaborates, "Choice, the unforeseeable exercise of free will, is underpinned by memory [...] and through our choices, the future is linked to the past [...] freedom consists in bringing duration, a consciousness of one's own becoming, to bear on being" (68). Or as Faiz puts it:

It is spring. And all at once have returned from the distant past
Those dreams, the youth
That had died on your lips
And after each death been born again.

Gilles Deleuze ([1966] 1991), building on Bergson, reiterated that human freedom is premised upon our ability to perceive time, not spatially, but in duration, or our ability to travel backwards and forwards in time in our imaginations. It is this perception of time as duration that opens up the present as the springboard of possibility from which individuals may redeem the past and invent an alternative future. It is a time-consciousness which is simultaneously aware of one's mortality and the possibility of exercising freedom in one's life. Collectively, it implies a historical consciousness that is aware of history as a cause and the sobering realization that humanity may itself become history. When this sense of time as duration becomes unhinged and we lose either memory or hope, life loses meaning.

In the following pages, I will read Marx to suggest that dialectical materialism is, as a method, imbued with a time-consciousness that counters the capitalistic severance of time. The concept of class struggle and praxis reconcile human action in the present with both the past and the future. Moreover, as a critique of capitalism, Marxism is well aware of its own historicity, and is as a theory both immanent and transcendent. Born of capitalism, Marxism holds the hope of becoming redundant in a postcapitalist future. Yet, it offers no narrative of progress, no guarantees that this will indeed be so. It therefore refuses the notion that novelty, which Peter Osborne (1995) has so well explained, is a core feature of capitalist modernity. Instead, by analyzing the structural logic of capitalism, Marx explained that the "new" in capitalism, that is, its unleashing of productive potential and unraveling of old hierarchies in favor of exchange relationships, had given way to recurrent economic crises based on exploitation and the commodity form. For Marx, the new – in the real sense of the word – was the end of the capitalism itself. The possibility of this happening remained contingent upon human action and/or class struggle, which must invariably happen in the present, i.e., at the level of history where space and time are integrally interconnected.[5]

At the same time, Marx launched a bitter critique of capitalism's cannibalization of worker's time, which he directly related to the loss of freedom and, ultimately, life itself. While capital treated labor as a commodity and cast itself as the creative element, Marx's fundamental point was that it was the working class that produced all value in society and that capital was nothing but "congealed" labor. Labor, he argued, created value (such as by unearthing raw materials or producing machinery), was the sole source of value (without human labor, including the imagination, the means of production such as raw materials or technology would remain lifeless), and when combined with others was capable of producing more than the sum of its parts. Capitalism, or the rule of private wealth, could only be maintained through overt force and an entire ideological edifice that denied the central role of labor and instead presented capital as the creative force in production.

Wages were a mechanism that disguised this contradiction between socialized labor and the private accumulation of wealth. On the surface, the wage appeared to be an exchange for the value created by labor, but in fact, the only way capital could be generated was by not paying labor its full measure. As Marx explained, profits rested on increasing the differential between the cost of labor, or the wages paid, and the profits generated by selling the products of social labor. This differential could be increased by lowering wages and/or increasing labor time. The bigger the differential, the greater the time the worker gave to the capitalist for free. As Engels ([1891] 2000) reiterated:

> In the present state of production, human labor-power not only produces in a day a greater value than it itself possesses and costs; but with each new scientific discovery, with each new technical invention, there also rises the surplus of its daily production over its daily cost, while as a consequence there diminishes that part of the working-day in which the laborer produces the equivalent of his day's wages, and, on the other hand, lengthens that part of the working-day in which he must present labor gratis to the capitalist.

Far more than being an equal return for labor given, Engels explains, wages were the costs the capitalists were willing to bear for the reproduction of the working class *as a whole* while incessantly trying to drive down those costs to bare minimum levels of subsistence. What those levels were depended upon local conditions and the balance of class struggle.

Critical to this claim was Marx's insight, also reiterated by Engels, that what the proletariat sell in exchange for wages is not labor but *labor-power*. Labor, Engels clarified, was, after all, inalienable from the laborer; it had literally "grown up with his person and is inseparable from it. [...] Its cost of production, therefore, coincides with his own cost of production; what the economist called the cost of production of labor is really the cost of production of the laborer, and therewith of his labor-power" (Engels [1891] 2000).

The wage, which appears on the surface to be the outcome of a free negotiation between consenting individuals, was, in fact, a cover for the parasitic exploitation that turns the labor of many into the wealth of the few.

As the neoliberal state withdraws from social welfare – compelling the working class to increasingly purchase its means of subsistence, such as water, electricity, food, schooling and health care – the burden on the wage and thus the exploitation of the working class is further exacerbated. In its neoliberal avatar, the ideology of the free market comes wrapped up in a radicalized obsession with entrepreneurialism – where everyone, even the poorest, are imagined as entrepreneurs. For instance, micro-credit eliminates the obligation for social welfare while simultaneously generating interest for the capitalists. Similarly, micro-commodities turn the hopes of abundance, egalitarianism, change and global citizenship embodied in consumer culture into profit-making ventures. For instance, when a single or small group of women apply for micro-credit to start a unit embroidering clothes for a multinational retail corporation, their labor not only generates profits for the corporation, but also for the financier making the initial loan. Similarly, micro-versions of global or premium brands of toothpastes, lotions and other consumer goods generate profits through economies of scale as well as prey on envy and a fascination with commodity culture as a means to social success. I will explore in greater detail the implications of this for the ways in which we imagine childhood. For now it will suffice to say that casting the poor as "consumers" of debt and micro-commodities is a neoliberal ploy meant to shed the last vestige of any remaining collective guilt on the part of the bourgeoisie. After all, if credit is available, why is there any need to exercise social responsibility? You can both "give" to the poor and profit from them at the same time.

Forced to sell their labor-power, that is, their time, the proletariat, Marx claimed, experienced their lifetime as being drained in the service of capital accumulation. The worker does not enter the market, Marx clarified, as a free agent free to "dispose" her or his time. Rather, capital is accumulated by driving down the costs of reproduction and the value of life of the working class as a *whole*. Take, for instance, the contemporary ability of capital to shift production anywhere in the world where labor is cheaper. Along with the structural unemployment that is characteristic of capital, this mobility further drives down the wages of all workers.

In fact, digital technology has further deepened capital's hunger for workers' time. Franco Berardi (2011) describes the process as the cellularization of the workforce – or gathering together workers from all over the world who are plugged in through mobile technologies such as the computer or the cell phone. Capital can now be made to pay only for that labor time, which it actually purchases – the rest of the time you work for free. Take for instance, young people hoping to break into the media industry. They put in hundreds of hours producing material for YouTube in the hopes that something will catch the public attention and, given enough hits, some corporate entity might buy their webspace for advertising. It is only then, when bought by capital, that they will finally start earning. While in Marx's day, the end of the work-day signaled the beginning of the worker's own time, the new flexible economy is increasingly obliterating that boundary.[6] Its implications are that life for the working class is increasingly experienced as an abstraction, a ticking clock with an impending expiration date. As Berardi (2011, 129) writes, "Strictly speaking, the workers no longer exist. Their time exists, their time is there, permanently available to connect, to produce in change for a temporary salary."

In capitalism, Marx had caustically commented, "[…] the period of time for which he [the worker] is free to sell his labor-power is the period of time for which he is forced to sell it" ([1867] 1976, 415). Marx's gothic images of capitalism – vampire-like sucking the blood and lifetime of living labor – and the significance of the battle over the eight-hour day suggest that he fully understood that time itself was at stake in the war between labor and capital.

> […] in fact, the vampire will not let go 'while there remains a single muscle, sinew of drop of blood to be exploited. For protection against the serpent of their agonies, the workers have to put their heads together and, as a class, compel the passing of a law, an all-powerful social barrier by which they can be prevented from selling themselves and their families into slavery and death by a voluntary contract with capital. In the place of the pompous catalogue of the 'inalienable rights of man' there steps the modest Magna Carta of the legally limited working day, which at last shall make clear when the time which the worker sells ends and when his own begins. *Quantum mutatus ab mol illo*/what a great change from that time (Virgil). (416; original emphasis and translation)

The Time of Capital and the Time of Parenting

The title of this introduction is taken from Marx's assertion that "*après moi le déluge*" (after me the flood) was "the watchword of every capitalist and every capitalist nation." It is the belief that disaster would strike someone else while I, having made my wealth, would escape. As Marx put it:

> In every stock-jabbing swindle everyone knows that some time or the other the crash must come, but everyone hopes that it may fall on the head of his neighbor, after he himself has caught the shower of gold and placed it in secure hands. ([1867] 1976, 381)

Because it is driven by the goal of accumulating private wealth, capital has "good reasons," Marx explained, to deny the sufferings of "legions of workers." It sees not humanity, but a mere resource, "an excess of population" to be used up, "plucked, so to speak, before they were ripe" (380). On the whole then, capital has complete disregard for human society as a whole and sustains a time-consciousness that is short-term and willing to abandon the future.[7] In bargaining with capital, what we get is a fragmented time consciousness which cannot reconcile the past with the future and remains in the frenzied grip of a vanishing present.

In bourgeois economics, the calculation of future costs against present gains is called, quite dispassionately, the "discount rate." Brett Clark, John Bellamy Foster and Richard York (2009) explain that the "discount rate" is the inverse of the compound interest. While compounding measures how much present-day investments will be worth in the future, discounting measures how much future benefits are worth today. They elaborate that such calculations are based on two moral issues: first, how much value we place on the welfare of future generations relative to the present; second, the extent to which we are prepared to sacrifice in the present for the future. Both considerations, it is obvious, rest on weighing the present against the future and the willingness to leave behind a more impoverished planet than the one inherited. In contrast to such present-centered calculations, the logic of parenting tends to think in the long-term lending itself to an ethic of saving, sacrificing, and postponing the pleasures of the present in favor of future generations. Although, there may well be an economic logic driven by personal gain here – investment in children is also seen as a form of insurance against old age – people routinely do put their children first with or without hopes of future returns.

In contrast to the long-term orientation of parenting, capitalism is structurally tied to the short-term. As David Harvey (2010) explains, speed is critical to capital accumulation. Survival in the market depends upon the speed with which invested capital is turned into profit and then reinvested as capital in an ever-increasing cycle. Capital that cannot be converted into profits, such as cars that cannot be sold or savings simply lying in the bank, is dead. While capitalists must factor the future in their calculations – for instance, mortgages are given with a view to recovering interest in the future – the system favors immediate returns to the long-term since the former not only keeps capital out of circulation, but also increases risk of loss.

There is another aspect to the temporality of capitalist accumulation which counters the future orientation of parenting: it is the promise of eternal youth, which saturates consumer culture, with its celebration of the market as an arena of freedom of choice. Youth is served up as a commodity for those who can afford to purchase it – cosmetics, clothes, drinks and vacations are all means to extend, recover, or remain forever young.[8] Portrayals of older people on vacations or in romantic relationships have emerged in advertising as well as in "Bollywood," a term I use in the same vein as Ashish Rajadhyaksha (2003), to speak of the culture industry aimed at bourgeois, cosmopolitan consumption. For instance, an ad for Coca-Cola in India shows four grey-haired women in a bright red car with colored bubbles around them, riding through the country. "We can't turn back the clock. But we will help you keep in touch with your childhood," says the ad copy. While these images are liberating, in that they grant the possibility of self-realization all through life, such self-realization is promised through the private consumption of commodities – a possibility constrained by one's purchasing power. Moreover, abandoning the future as a whole produces fears that surface in dystopian apocalyptic imaginations of some future disaster.

There may be observed, in the contemporary middle-class Indian family, a palpable anxiety about an uncertain future that is expressed in an increasingly curtailed regimen around preparing children for the labor market. Coaching academies for speaking English, interviews for admission to kindergarten, an inordinate emphasis on information technology in schools and prep schools that consider the arts as a means to increase one's marketability in the future indicate that the majority of Indian children are being integrated into capital, not as consumers, but as labor. In fact, the advertisers are well aware of this and offer their commodities as a means to secure advantage in this race into the future. Take for instance the copy from a Nestle ad that advises, "If you want your child to be a champion tomorrow […] start today."

The parent who holds on to the idealized notion of childhood as a *time to be free* and to be passed in play, can, in fact, appear to harm the child within this regimen, causing her or him to fall behind in the race. In other words, as the process of proletarianization, understood as the cannibalization of time, sinks lower and lower as childhood itself is eroded and the person(s) charged with teaching this time-discipline are none other than the parents and caregivers, children, often eager to please parents, internalize this discipline and, filled with shame and guilt, make painful choices, such as that between studying for exams or sleeping.

While instilling such time-discipline appears, on the surface, to be a private dilemma to be sorted out within the family, reading Marx can help locate the root of this painful conflict in the structure of capitalism. Capitalist development, Marx argues, depends upon turning publicly held resources (the commons, water, etc.) into privately owned commodities to be put up for sale, the exploitation of labor and its conversion into a commodity and a systemic tendency towards monopoly that produces islands of extravagance in a sea of poverty. In other words, capitalism expands through an ongoing process of privatizing, enclosing, and dispossessing what was either socially owned or socially produced. This is the basis of the culture of the risk, where everyone, including children, confronts others as antagonists.

Arrested Development and the Dispossession of Lifetime

In the Latin America of the '60s and '70s – the home of the first experiments in neoliberalism – capitalist development was characterized as the "Development of Underdevelopment." Now visible on a world stage as neoliberalism, the full implications of this theory, that is its critique of the *underdevelopment of capitalist development* and the inadequacy of economic indices such as gross national product (GNP) as measures of growth (rather than social criterion such as standards of health, education, opportunities for self-development) are becoming clearer. For instance, Andre Gunder Frank cited his fifteen-year-old son's characterization of Margaret Thatcher's England as an "underdeveloping country" (1991). I find this insight very useful in elaborating on the nature of development that has accompanied neoliberalism and will argue that the moral panics surrounding the rapid sexualization or "growing-up" of children and young people in India are a response to the integration of the young as both labor and buyers in the global economy as well as the commodification of youth.

Moreover, the characterization of capitalism as a form of arrested development is also an appropriate term to describe the nature of subjectivities favored by neoliberalism. In particular, I identify the production of lumpen subjectivities as a key component of both socializing young people into capitalism as well as the moral crisis that surrounds it. Wendy Brown (2003), following Michel Foucault's notion of governmentality, has suggested that what is new about neoliberalism is the production of a self-regulating subject whose entire being is suffused by market rationality:

> It [neoliberalism] figures individuals as rational, calculating creatures whose moral autonomy is measured by their capacity for "self-care" – the ability to provide for their own needs and service their own ambitions. In making the individual fully responsible for her/himself, neo-liberalism equates moral responsibility with rational action; it relieves the discrepancy between economic and moral behavior by configuring morality entirely as a matter of rational deliberation about costs, benefits, and consequences. In so doing, it also carries responsibility for the self to new heights: the rationally calculating individual bears full responsibility for the consequences of his or her action no matter how severe the constraints on this action, e.g., lack of skills, education, and childcare in a period of high unemployment and limited welfare benefits.

Such subjectivity requires a serious modification in the relationship between adults and children, particularly within the middle-class family that extends childhood until, in many cases, the "child" marries and sets up his or her own family. In turn, children owe it to their parents to take care of them in old age. The calculating, amoral subject of neoliberalism must, however, use the family and discard it when it appears to be a burden. The social anxieties demanded of such individualization are the subject of television melodramas that dominate Indian television these days. There is also a new culture of religiosity that aims to soothe the loneliness borne of confrontations with an increasingly volatile market.

However, market rationality has, I will argue, also slid into subjectivities that are better described as lumpen. Marx, used the term lumpen, or the dregs/shreds of discarded cloth, to characterize both those on the lowest rungs of the proletariat – the homeless, the petty criminals who did not produce surplus value through wage labor – and the very elite who "get rich not by production, but by pocketing the already available wealth of others" (2003, 37–8). Marx explained in relation to mid-nineteenth century France that, at the very top, the finance bourgeoisie, like the petty thief at the bottom, make money by swindling, speculation, scams, and a calculated use of others for profit in which the bourgeoisie would not hesitate to break its own rules. This recurrent feature of capital may now be observed in the most recent and radicalized phase of financialization when, at its highest level, money is generated via the circulation of money as commodity (see Amiya Bagchi 2006). The sub-prime mortgages, Ponzi schemes, kickbacks, frauds and other such forms of speculation and gambling are the official culture of lumpen capitalism worldwide.

Capitalism has brought in its wake in India, with our own patriarchal traditions, a fascination with a lumpen sort of masculinity with the lumpen appearing as the doppelganger or much desired "other" of middle-class masculinity in "Bollywood."[9] In films such as *Good Boy, Bad Boy* (Chaudhary 2007), *Tashan* (Style) (Acharya 2008) and *Rab Ne Bana di Jodi* (God Has Made Us One) (Chopra 2008), the terribly ordinary, but upwardly mobile, middle-class young man learns to succeed and at the same time get the girl by learning to con, swindle, and flex his muscle. These lumpen subjectivities are experienced as a breakdown of the social fabric, including the family and relationship between generations.

Capitalism and Childhood

Capitalism remains now, as when Karl Marx described it a century-and-a-half ago, an entire system with profound consequences for how we live, love, work, and, quite simply, be human. The notion of childhood and youth as a time of play was an invention of capitalist modernity. It was on the basis of the abundance generated by social labor that childhood could be imagined as a state of *becoming* not being.[10] Given the right opportunities, it could be argued, all children could reach their true potential and it became socially abhorrent to see children laboring in factories or on the streets. Not that it ever took hold for the vast majority of Indian children, neoliberalism is rapidly eroding this notion of childhood as an unfolding or a state of becoming and, unashamedly for its talk of the new twenty-first century, knitting children's futures with the accidental circumstances of birth and fate.

Neoliberal withdrawals of social welfare have, as Jeremy Seabrook (2001) discusses, reached the backs of working-class children with a new force – feeding off their labor, their childhoods and their very lives (see also Robert Weil 2008). Much of Marx's most bitter critique of capital concerned its exploitation of working-class children and underlays his call to workers to organize against child labor, to act:

> [...] as a class, [to] compel the passing of a law [restricting the hours of children's labor] as an all-powerful social barrier by which they can be prevented from selling themselves and their families into slavery and death by voluntary contract with capital. ([1867] 1976, 416)

No essentialist, Marx deconstructed the notion of childhood as a social construct well ahead of the postmodernists. However, in contrast to the postmodern and poststructuralist penchant for "different regimes of truth," Marx explained that the experience of childhood was contingent upon the battle between labor and capital. He mocked the "anthropology of the capitalists" haggling over whether childhood ended at 10 or 11 years of age, or "[...] the age limit of the *category of human beings who, under the name of children*" were to be restricted to eight hours of work ([1867] 1976, 392; emphasis added). Evocative of Jonathan Swift's (1729) "A Modest Proposal" that the best use Irish landlords could get out of the children of the poor was to eat them, having "already devoured most of the parents," Marx had this to say about silk manufacturers putting children aged 11–13 to ten-hour working days:

> The children were quite simply slaughtered for the sake of their delicate fingers, just as horned cattle are slaughtered in Southern Russia for their hides and their fat. ([1867] 1976, 406)

Marx explained that child labor performed an economic function for capital – children were cheaper than adults (they were not paid at all during the first six months they worked as apprentices), lightened the workload for adult workers, and, finally, depressed wages as a whole by increasing the supply of cheap labor in the market.

Marx's analysis of the uses of child labor for capital is just as pertinent in India today. A few years ago in 2007, when it was discovered that clothes for the international outfit Gap were being produced in a sweatshop in New Delhi by children working 16-hour days in conditions akin to slavery, Kamal Nath, the then minister for commerce, chastised the nongovernmental organizations (NGOs) for bad publicity. In other words, it was the exploitation of children that gave India the competitive edge in the global market (see J. Kapur 2007). Ironically, while capitalists seek to maximize their profits in the present, they are entirely comfortable postponing benefits to labor until a future, undefined date.

Ultimately, Marx explained the fight over restricting the work-day for children was part of an ongoing "civil war" between labor and capital. He went on to describe the long working hours prescribed by the Printmakers Act of 1845 – 16 hours for women and children aged 8–13, unlimited hours for men over 13 years of age – as "parliamentary abortion" ([1867] 1976, 408). Antonella Picchio (1992) has argued that the state and the family are the two sites where the battles between labor and capital are fought out, lived through, won, and lost (see also Luxton 2006; Brenner and Laslett 1991). Elaborating on how neoliberalism is concretely manifested in the experience of childhood and youth, Henry Giroux (2009, x–xi) writes that young people have become disposable and expendable and we have been living through a "war on youth" for the last 30 years. As capital has become ever more mobile, the necessity of investing in social welfare has diminished. The costs are heavy at both ends of the human life cycle, that is, childhood and old age – when human beings are most dependent on others.

Reading Cultural Texts

While policy discussions regarding neoliberalism have tended to slide into abstractions, it is in journalistic accounts, essays, popular fiction, cinema and television that one can find depictions of the hidden, experiential and subjective aspects of these battles between labor and capital. As E. P. Thompson declared, "there is no such thing as economic growth which is not, at the same time growth or change of a culture" (1967, 97). The human ability to understand and resist is at the core of Marx's idea of class-consciousness and it is in cultural artifacts that we can discern subjectivities resistant to and amenable to neoliberalism. Like Marx, we must turn to poets, storytellers, journalists, myths and beliefs to describe the world we live in and to political economy to understand its structures – with the certain knowledge that we are not condemned to living in its humanly constructed structures forever. The sub-title of Marx's *Capital* was, after all, *A Critique of Political Economy*.

The Battle at Home and in the Market

I will try in these pages to trace the politics of time and the image of the new "global generation" that is emerging in popular discourses – moving freely across film, television, print and consumer culture – and show how the social construction of childhood and youth is a battleground between labor and capital. The battle is plain to see. It is particularly volatile in the professional middle class, which is the most insecure about its ability to maintain its place in the social hierarchy. Relying mainly on professional capital as a means of advancement, the middle class must put its children through a rigorous training and educational process, whose success relies on the degree to which the child imbibes the lessons of delayed gratification.

This basic middle-class value is now in conflict with the entire gamut of advertising and marketing that promotes immediate gratification as freedom and the hallmark of youth identity – all in the midst of escalating inequality and social antagonism. So, if on the one hand one can observe a public sphere where the young are exercising greater sexual, as well as other, life choices, there is also an extraordinary degree of violence against it. The extreme examples of this are the honor killings of young couples who dare cross caste lines, sanctioned by the khap panchayats.[11] As a khap sympathizer, Dr. Santosh Dahiya (Vrinda 2010), explained to the press, "The parents kill their children due to the shame they are bringing to the home [...] What can a khap do?" The brutal contradictions of capitalist concentration of wealth are disastrous for relations within the family as well as among men and women. If the air-conditioned, heavily guarded mall and multiplex promises a certain freedom of sexual expression, there is right outside the threat of sexual harassment, rape and kidnappings to act as a terror tactic to enforce the submission to patriarchal and caste hierarchies.

If, on the one hand, school counselors and films like *3 Idiots* (Hirani 2009) tell parents to act as facilitators who help their children find their own calling in life, the pressures on children to obey and submit to authority are immense. On 21 April 2010, Indian television broke a news story about children 6–16 years old in a school in Surat, Gujarat, who were made to walk, in the presence of parents, on hot coals and broken glass as a way to "build self-confidence."[12] The powerful appeal of the call to lose the self in violent, fascist projects such as honor killings or the coal walking experiment can be understood from this young student's explanation for why he walked on coals: "I was afraid but when people who teach you and you look up to say that there is nothing to be afraid of, you do not feel fear."[13]

The Book in Outline

I begin, in Chapter 1, "Brand India's Biggest Sale: The Cultural Politics and Political Economy of India's 'Global Generation,'" by taking on the dominant narrative that neoliberalism has given birth to a new "global generation," a marketing term used to celebrate a generation that shares, to an unprecedented degree, a common consumer culture comprised of global media and brands. I discuss the class-based nature of the integration of young people into global capital, both as labor and consumers and the ways in which it produces a discourse around generations – the class interests that underlie India's turn towards neoliberalism – and argue that India's young people are the key commodity put up for sale by Brand India on the market shelves of global capital.

In Chapter 2, "Arrested Development and the Making of a Neoliberal State," I elaborate on the shift to Brand India as a withdrawal from the development functions of the state and a deepening of the arrested development characteristic of capitalism – both of society as a whole and the individuals within it. The neoliberal state is, I will indicate, a continuation of the class politics of the postcolonial state and not its alternative. Nevertheless, it is a radicalization of uneven development in every sense of the term. Building on Wendy Brown's (2003) insight that neoliberalism justifies market rationality as the new morality, I will discuss the ways in which this informs the political project of the Hindu fundamentalist movement, known as *Hindutva* and resonates with a sense of time derived from an absolute relativism in moral reasoning. The amoralism of the market valorizes the atomistic, enterprising individual as well lumpen subjectivities, which the religious Right draws upon in fascist ideologies of submission to some higher authority evoking a time-consciousness in which individual human life is merely the manifestation of an absolute timelessness.

In Chapter 3, "For Some Dreams a Lifetime is Not Enough: The Rasa Aesthetic and the Everyday in Neoliberalism," I turn to the experience of time in capital, in that capitalism enforces a disciplinary regime in which time is a mere means of generating profits to be used up in the production or consumption of market-produced commodities. Neoliberalism has radicalized such instrumentalization of time even further. In fact, Hollywood cinema, the cultural form par excellence of the American century, has long served as a training ground in such sensibility. Here, I discuss popular Bombay cinema as a kind counter-narrative to such a disciplinary regimen and argue that the recent popularity of "Bollywood" is both a consequence of this alternative aesthetic as well as its accommodation to Hollywood style narratives that stage individual dramas in a space enclosed away from history. I also do a close reading of one popular Indian television soap, *Pavitra Rishta* (The Pure Relationship) (Joshi and Latkar 2010), to discuss how television soaps restore an awareness of cyclical time to the everyday and serve as a coping mechanism for the radicalized speed-up and fragmentation of time in neoliberalism.

Chapter 4, "An 'Arranged Love' Marriage: India's Neoliberal Turn and the 'Bollywood' Wedding Culture Industry," takes the trend of extravagant weddings currently popularized by Indian popular cinema and a burgeoning industry in weddings, as a case in point to discuss the new morality around consumption. I argue that the "Bollywood" wedding is a specific class-based gendered response to India's turn to neoliberalism. It is symptomatic of the neoliberal subject, who must mark its "arrival" by individuating, packaging, and presenting the self as a unique individual even when performing something as conventional as a "traditional wedding."

Chapter 5, "*Ek Haseenah Thi* (There Once Was a Maiden): The Vanishing Middle Class and Other Neoliberal Thrills," discusses the emergence of a new genre – the conspiracy thriller – in popular Hindi cinema as a cultural response to neoliberalism. Fredric Jameson (1992) has described the conspiracy genre as a "poor person's mapping of the postmodern age," the response of an imaginary befuddled by the "social totality that is global capitalism in formal or representational terms." Its aesthetics of speed, movement and surprise express the fear and furious reasoning of an individual who must save her- or himself from a conspiracy that threatens to destroy them. I contextualize the genre in the urban spaces of neoliberalism, its architecture of private enclosures and the paranoid subjectivities in particular middle-class anxieties around gender as well as loss of class position.

Capital does not and cannot reproduce itself smoothly. Marx's dialectical understanding shows us that capitalism carries the seeds of its own destruction. Therefore, just as it must integrate a new generation to oil its mechanisms, it must also produce a generation that resists it. Moreover, its narrative of endless novelty cannot render obsolete – like its commodities – the memories of a previous generation. While researching what gave children and young people the courage to act in the US civil rights movement, Robert Coles (1986) made the significant discovery that it was an "uncanny blend of memory and desire; a chance to struggle for a new situation that holds a large promise, while earning along the way the approval of one's parents, neighbors friends, and not the least, oneself" that empowered young people to stand up against domination (35). In other words, inter-generational solidarity can dissolve personal anxieties and create an environment in which to struggle is to become whole. Or, put differently, if hope lies in the future, in the imagined end of unbearable pain, courage is drawn from the past, from memories of previous struggles.

Much too often we have been taught to view youth rebellion as a revolt against the older generation, a kind of oedipal narrative of the young breaking free of patriarchal tradition. In doing so, we deny the centrality of history, memory and continuity in anti-imperialist, working-class struggles; as if the contradiction between labor and capital has already been settled. In order to reproduce its relations, capital must integrate another generation into its fold. Yet, it is this very process that poses a two-fold threat to the legitimacy of the neoliberal state. First, it calls for a profound transformation in moral economy, asking that we give up on the future and stop saving for our children. Second, it must erase the lingering memories of the anti-colonial movement by claiming that selling the nation as a brand is the epitome of nationalism when the inequalities within the nation are at an all-time high. The former robs the future while the latter is an assault on memory.

Chapter 1

BRAND INDIA'S BIGGEST SALE: THE CULTURAL POLITICS AND POLITICAL ECONOMY OF INDIA'S "GLOBAL GENERATION"

Capital demands more youthful workers, fewer adults.

—Karl Marx[1]

Outsourcing is a story of the past. We now want people to see India as a manufacturing base, as the youngest nation with fortunate future demographics.

—Indian minister of commerce Kamal Nath[2]

Ever since the Indian state officially turned to neoliberalism in 1991, it has also became commonplace in business-bureaucratic policy to speak of the nation as "Brand India," "India Inc." or "India Shining." Brand India is the favored term of choice for the Congress Party – the party currently in power with Prime Minister Manmohan Singh. The Bharatiya Janata Party (BJP), the political party previously in power with an openly Hindu fundamentalist agenda, preferred India Shining. Regardless of the specific nomenclature, what this represents is the MBAization of governance, such that the nation is imagined as a brand to be marketed, positioned, and sold on the global market. There is a revolving door between the government and the International Monetary Fund (IMF) and World Bank, from Prime Minister Manmohan Singh, who earlier worked at the World Bank, to Raghuram Rajan, the current chief economic advisor at the Indian Ministry of Finance and a previous chief economist and director of research at the IMF. This is a retreat from the liberal-democratic conception of the state as the voice of its citizens and compelled, even if minimally, to enact certain measures of social welfare. It is also a withdrawal from the notion of the post-independence development state, according to which the state was supposed to take an activist role in ensuring equity, justice and economic development aimed at securing national self-reliance. Instead, the defining objective of Brand India is to position the nation as a market for consumer goods, a competitive source of cheap labor and a lucrative investment opportunity for global capital.

The brainchild of state and commerce, the concept of Brand India is an invention of the India Brand Equity Foundation (IBEF), which, in turn, is a collaborative venture between the Confederation of Indian Industry (CII) and the Indian Ministry of Commerce. What is significant here is not so much the nomenclature – because Brand India is also variously described as India, Inc. – but that it represents a shift in orientation towards the nation, which is now imagined as a commodity to be marketed to global capital and it is thus that the term has a cache beyond IBEF. Brand India's self-described mission is to position India as an attractive place to do business with and business in.[3] One of its core selling points or Unique Selling Point (USP) is the new "global generation." Also known as the "children of liberalization," these under-thirty-year-olds are celebrated for their ability to work hard and long as well as for their "world-class" consuming habits. They are the basis for claiming that India has shed its former Third World status to become a global power.

In fact, the rhetoric around the "global generation" and its unlimited appetite for purchasing global brands and media culture is one of the key justifications of neoliberalism.[4] The association with young people helps present neoliberalism as something new rather than a radicalized version of capitalism while the emphasis on buying rather than laboring presents it as an ongoing promise of freedom. Take, for instance, the following write-up on shoe styles in the magazine section of a national daily:

> The 21st century has brought about a sea change in the aspirations of the average Indian consumers. [...] For the first time, they have a choice. A choice of what they drive, what they eat and drink, and what they wear. And this choice is not dictated by what is available in the [local] market but what they choose to buy. [...] Take the case of footwear. Young people are becoming increasingly sophisticated in their shoe preferences. [...] Gucci, Testoni, Berluti, Emilio Pucchi, and Roberto Cavalli [...] have made stylish footwear a part of their wardrobe essentials. (Shivshankar, 2012)

Since the 1990s, global brands have become ubiquitous in India and, in keeping with their counterparts in the affluent nations, Indian children and young people are being initiated into a network of commodities through, what Beryl Langer (2004) so accurately characterizes as, the "commoditoy." The term demystifies the toy of its associations with childhood. While giving a toy may well be an expression of parental love and the toy itself offers possibilities of play, the term "commoditoy" is a clear reminder that children's toys are systemically integrated in the economic (profit-making) and cultural (commodification of life) logic of capital. According to Langer (2011, 9):

> The essential feature of a 'commoditoy' is the capacity to stimulate rather than satisfy desire; satiation is endlessly postponed. Each act of consumption is a beginning rather than an end, the first or next step in an endless series for which each particular toy is an advertisement, first because its package is also a catalogue and second because it is part of a tantalizing universe without which the one just purchased is incomplete. Children's sense of sufficiency is continuously undermined because the moment of possession is also the beginning of desire. In consequence, the volume of material objects accumulated in the course of a 'normal' Western childhood has multiplied exponentially.

"Commoditoys" integrate the child into the branded life, tying self-worth and value to one's purchasing power, that is, one's place in the market. Advertising rests on deepening feelings of envy, competitiveness and ceaseless dissatisfaction. Yet, branding makes complete sense as a business strategy in a market saturated with homogenous commodities that must incessantly differentiate from each other. It is, after all, the mark "Barbie" that distinguishes the Mattel, Inc. property from another cheaply produced one. Moreover, the brand allows for the production of a concept around which contemporary mega-corporate entities can cross-promote their products.

The marketing term for generating a web of commodities is "synergy" and it is driven by the need to maximize profits by translating a brand across multiple platforms such that products constantly advertise one another. Some examples of such super-brands to hit the Indian market recently are Funskool, a toy-manufacturer licensed with the television channel Cartoon Network to market *Powerpuff Girls* merchandizing. So, now you have an entire network of commodities around a children's television channel. You don't only watch *Powerpuff Girls* on television; you can buy t-shirts, jewelry, buttons, toy figures, umbrellas, footwear and even iPhone cases with the Powerpuff logo. Similarly, Mattel, a toy company, markets Batman toy figures and action games and Barbie dolls and movies. Zee Network, an India-based television channel, has, in collaboration with the Essar group, franchised preschool education with its KidZee centers where the curriculum is based almost entirely on media characters and toys and a concept cynically titled "Entertaining Education" (Indiantelevision.com 2005). Cartoon Network, which is owned by Time Warner, Inc., sells both toys and theme parks like Cartoon Network Townsville and Planet Pogo. These theme parks, or "Family Entertainment Centers" in marketing jargon, have turned family get-togethers into venues for lessons in brand awareness.

Birthday parties amongst middle- to upper-middle-class families in cities like Bombay or Delhi serve as major venues for the enactment of childhood around these market-produced networks of commodities. The work of organizing birthdays is now outsourced by parents to event managers who, picking a media-related theme such as Spider-Man, launch a buying spree of costumes for both guests and hosts and props that are integrated into the party and return gifts to be exchanged at the end of the party. A friend of mine, who threw a party for her four-year-old not revolving around a theme, laughingly described it as "old-fashioned." The outsourced birthday party is far more a site for displaying class distinction and geared towards generating adult envy rather than enabling children's play. Mothers told me about children as young as two and three having to be forced into costumes and dragged in protest to parties.

One of the most embarrassing sights at such parties is the line-up of young girls – from poor, often tribal, backgrounds and barely out of puberty themselves, who take care of these children on a day-to-day basis – sitting along the walls while the DJs coax parents to play with their children. Since childcare, such as bathing, feeding, or dressing up, is commonly passed on to hired help in middle- and upper-middle-class households, both time and a reason for play between parents and children has to be invented.

Yet, it is not that middle-class parents are uninvolved in their children's lives. If anything, observers, including Katharina and Sudhir Kakkar (2007), have noted that parents' involvement, even within extended families, has intensified. Joint families, albeit still a common living arrangement, are now smaller often with only one son and his family living in the parental home. Such families are better understood as nuclear families living together where the intimate relationship between the couple is recognized as primary, and the responsibility of child rearing rests with the parents rather than being shared with the grandparents.

The Kakkars (2007, 68) observe that the contemporary middle-class woman who is more educated, mobile and often pursuing her own career tends to be even more child-centered and identified with the achievements, especially educational, of her children than her traditional counterpart. New technologies, including cell phones, have strengthened the ability of mothers to keep tabs on children and also remain in constant touch with them. For instance, I observed a mother texting her son with praise for his performance in a school play as soon as he got off the stage. The performance not yet over, he texted back, "thx."

There is also an observable increase in one-child households and I found that parents frequently used the word "investment" to refer to their only child, as in explaining the choice to take large loans to send the child abroad for study or for the mother taking a break from her career to raise the child. Articulating a typical concern, a mother told me that she would never have a second child because she did not want her single child to "feel less" in any way by the certain "division of attention and resources" that a second child would bring about. Parents regularly speak of the increasing expense of raising children as a direct outcome of the escalation of the costs of commodities now available in the market "for" children. Buying these commodities is seen as a necessary investment, both to forestall the child's feelings of inadequacy and to ensure upward mobility in a future that is closely tied with parental security in old age.

Consequently, the expenditure on children's commodity culture is not so much directed towards gratification as it is towards a disciplinary regime of preparing for success in the future, globalized job market and insuring the parents' own future relationship with the child. As "investment" in children's futures, parental expenditures on children's commodity culture are a form of control over a child in the present. Since children do not earn income and depend upon the parent for access to the consumer market, it is inevitable that they would feel a certain sense of gratitude towards the parent – a debt that underlies the child's obligation to the parent and concomitant feelings of guilt and rage when the "investment" is asserted.

Children frequently justify their purchases, especially the higher cost items, by arguing that they would help them do better in school. For instance, it would be impressed upon the parent that a Scooty at Rs. 50,000 would make it easier for the child to make it on time to his or her tutor's lessons after school or that a BlackBerry at around Rs. 10,000 would make it possible to confer with others in completing homework. In my discussions with children, I found them eager to prove themselves as self-regulating and obedient – a tendency that was, perhaps, encouraged further by my graying hair. While children often recounted pranks played on teachers as a group, individually they tended to overwhelmingly present themselves as worried about schoolwork and opposed to spontaneous bursts of activity. For instance, an offer to go to a movie during the school week, even when there was no homework pending, would be first turned down before being accepted after permission was obtained from a parent.

There is a certain performance routine expected of "good" school-going children around commodity culture. They must first appear to reject its attractions before they may be persuaded to reluctantly go along with the fun, albeit on the goading of adults. Once that role-play would be over and done with children would indeed live in the moment, savoring the break from the disciplinary routines. Such forbiddance of commodity culture and the parental hold over expenses deepens the attractions of the commodity, tying its pleasures to freedom from childhood itself. A young man in his late twenties, now living on his own as a professional, thoughtfully replied to my open-ended question about how he remembered his childhood in an urban, upper-middle-class family with, "you were not allowed to make mistakes."

The standards of perfection imposed on "investments" are deeply internalized. They put young children in the impossible position of see-sawing between the paradoxical uses of children's commodity culture both as an assertion of individual choice and parental control. The point I am trying to make here is twofold: first, children's commodity culture has stepped into and helped reinforce the space created by the increased nuclearization, both real and psychological, of the middle-class family; second, the middle-class home, especially the mother–child team, is the key site for the social reproduction of labor.[5] The very same commodities that promise spontaneity and individual expression to children as consumers are also manifestations of parental investment in children and thus serve as tools for discipline and conformism. They turn into object lessons for a time-consciousness in which life is lived entirely in anticipation of returns to be realized in the future and so, perhaps, never lived at all.

Reproducing Future Labor: The Home and the Market

It was the bourgeois home – sustained on social labor – that could provide the time and space necessary for the invention of childhood as a stage free from labor and its idealization as a site of possibility. Over the course of the first half of the twentieth century, the attributes associated with childhood, that is, spontaneity and freedom, were extended to young people as well. Imagined as the opposite of the public world of the market, the private sphere, centered on the home, was idealized as the space of leisure, authenticity and freedom from work. The product of social labor, Peter Osborne (1995, 192) observes dialectically, is that the private was imagined as the opposite of social labor and invested with utopian and romantic possibilities.

As Henri Lefebvre (1995) reminds us, the association between youth or childhood and the accompanying openness towards the present is a specific feature of capitalist modernity. It stems from a historical consciousness in which time is no longer perceived as naturally repetitive and the past no longer dominates the present. He writes:

> We should never forget how far the human world in its youth was innocent and naïve, immersed as it was in the ever-renewed rhythms of nature, yet how startlingly devoid of youth it was. (165)

Hindu epics are filled with tales extolling the virtues of the young sacrificing for the old. The most striking in this genre is the story of Yayati from the

Mahabharata. Yayati was a powerful king, who was one day cursed with immediate decrepitude unless a young man willingly took the curse upon himself. It turned out that there was no one in the kingdom other than his own son, Pooru, who was ready to make such a supreme sacrifice. Pooru's acceptance of his father's curse is made even more poignant by the fact that he made the pact on his wedding night. Ultimately though, Yayati took back the curse upon himself and Pooru was restored to his youth. Although the story acknowledges the pain of the loss of youth, it nevertheless underlies the assumption that children's lives belong to the parents, in particular the father.

The idea of childhood or youth as the site of possibility from where a new future may be imagined was made possible by the modern sense of self that emerged with the bourgeois revolutions. It was premised on the abundance generated by social labor which made it possible to imagine that a large majority of human beings could in childhood be free from labor. Thus, children came to be imagined as blank slates and childhood, later extended to youth, considered phases in life when one was free from the demands of the market. Most certainly, it was only the bourgeois child who was granted this openness in the early twentieth century and also under a forced regimen of deliberate distancing from knowledge of sex and commerce. For the proletariat, it was not until 1938 that child labor was abolished in its entirety in the US and childhood was enforced by deliberate seclusion in children's homes, where working-class children's knowledge and experience of the world was wiped out in the bid to produce a "proper" childhood.

In India, childhood arrived in the midst of the making of the colonial middle class, already formed as a little adult. Limited by colonial rule from rising in the military, political, and entrepreneurial hierarchy, the colonial middle class, Sumit Sarkar (1997) explains, found an education in English indispensable for the respectable professions of lawyers, teachers, journalists, writers, government officials or clerks. Childhood in the Indian middle class has historically been tied to an ethic of labor and a disciplined use of time – a link that remains unbroken despite the new language of immediate gratification surrounding children's consumer culture today.[6]

If in early twentieth century, portraits of the lone child in Western photography heightened the spontaneity and temporariness of childhood children in India were squarely placed within the family and in accordance with the hierarchies within it. As Christopher Pinney (2008) notes, it was much easier – due to lighting and the longer times required for registering an image – to compose a photograph around an individual or a couple, a fact that, Pinney elaborates, was constitutive of and helped build a modern subjectivity. However, both Indian photographers and subjects continued to

Figure 2. Women and children from an extended family. Note the youngest, and perhaps the most recent bride, at the feet with her infant on the floor. Required to sit still for the length of the shot – a task impossible for infants and toddlers – the children move and "spoil" the picture.

Figure 3. The hierarchies are even stronger here and the separation between men and children strictly maintained.

Figure 4. And here the lone male child, a little adult occupying his place in the male hierarchy.

Figure 5. More in line with the Victorian family portrait, this photograph suggests movement through depth. Note the vase and the table on the side and the bookshelf in the back. Yet, the children look back, like the mother, unsmiling.

pose the extended family despite these technical difficulties and in these early photographs the child who moved scrambled the picture.

The sex-segregation within the extended middle-class Indian family and the placement of children in the women's arena was another reason for the formality with which children are posed in these early photographs. Sudhir Kakkar (1978) and Katharina Kakkar (Kakkar and Kakkar 2007) elaborate on the reluctance among parents, especially fathers, towards playing with their own children in the traditional household. Cohesion within the joint family, that is, where brothers stayed together after marriage in the paternal home, Sudhir and Katharina Kakkar explain, rested upon undermining the smaller, nuclear unit within the larger family. Expressions of attachment, especially sexual, were strongly discouraged amongst couples and playing with one's own child in the shared spaces of the joint family was perceived as flaunting that private, sexual relationship to others. Because motherhood was traditionally defined as the highest objective of a woman's life and childcare was performed within the women's sphere of sex-segregated households, expressions of intimacy between women and children were socially sanctioned and, in fact, celebrated. In contrast, the public spaces of the household, such as those framed by the family portrait, were marked by hierarchical and restrained relationships between children and adults.

A core concern of Marxist-feminist and social reproduction theory has been to analyze the reproduction of labor itself, or what Marx and Engels had described as *labor-power*.[7] In this vein, Antonella Picchio (1992) has argued that the state and the family are the two sites where the battles between labor and capital are fought out, lived through, won, and lost. Put differently, capital does not stop at the door-step of the household leaving it free to raise children in any way it would wish. Rather, the choices a family makes are tied to its class position and the very nature of the family is intertwined with the specific nature of social relations between capital and labor at that time.

With the shift towards neoliberalism, the middle-class home in India has emerged increasingly, not as a site of leisure or freedom from work, but rather as a sweatshop for the reproduction of labor for the global market, albeit the labor is performed within the household and appears disguised as consumption and is, therefore, more pleasurable. I emphasize that noting the economic function of the household in capital is not to deny the genuine feelings of love and concern amongst families nor the potential within the private sphere of the family to, as Walter Benjamin remarked, "try out in advance" relations not yet permissible in capitalism (in Eagleton 1981). In fact, it is exactly this painful contradiction between the idealized autonomy of the private sphere and its very real dependence upon and assimilation into the market that produces one of the deepest felt crises in capitalism.

One of the most visible manifestations of such crisis is the diminished time for play in middle-class homes. The increasing pressures of time in two-career households and the availability of cheap, domestic labor has seriously curtailed the likelihood of combining daily routines of childcare, such as bathing, feeding, etc., with play. Leaving all this work to hired help, parents and, in particular, mothers, turn the time that parents do have with their children into drill sessions focused on coping with and mastering schoolwork.

There is now an entire small-scale industry that services the increased demands placed by schools on domestic time. School projects that could have been fun because they combine tactile work as well as intellectual – creating a model of the solar system or filling in maps, for example – are now outsourced to stationary shops in neighborhoods that then pass it on to home-based workers. Even assignments from preschools such as putting together a costume of an animal or fictional character are regularly outsourced. On the one hand, this practice is driven by an amplified competition amongst mothers over their children's performance in school that makes home-produced work appear amateurish in comparison with professional creations. On the other hand, schools, in a bid to outdo each other in showcasing the productivity of their students and staff, have escalated their demands on students, thus putting a real squeeze on the time available at home. Competition is the motor that drives both families and schools and it is now in overdrive.

Consequently, play has become synonymous with time carved outside of domestic routines in vacations or other venues of consumption. These spaces are then filled by super-brands driven by the powerful ambition to transform children's play, education and, more generally, culture itself into a profit generating exercise by directing it towards the consumption of "commoditoys."

A Very Profitable Thing Called Youth

The ambition of turning every experience and aspect of life into a commodity to be bought and sold is a systemic feature of capitalism. What Langer's concept of the "commoditoy" captures so well is the central function of commodification in the economic and cultural logic of capitalism. The commodity, Marx claimed ([1867] 1976, 163) was a very "queer" thing. Taking the example of a coat, Marx explained that its value emerged not simply from its use-value, that is, its ability to

Figure 6. Shopping as play. The Oberoi Mall in Bombay represents itself as the space of freedom away from work where everyone, including children, can be children. Photo © the author.

keep someone warm. Rather, in the capitalist marketplace, its value arose from the amount of "abstract labor time" invested in its production (151). Denying this relationship between the producer and purchaser, or turning labor-time itself into a commodity, the coat appears on market shelves as an autonomous entity in competition with others. This transformation of a relationship into a thing, of putting differing prices on people's time, was, Marx noted, nothing less than "magic and necromancy" (169).

These commodities then have to be sold and capitalist expansion requires an ever-escalating process of commodification under which new markets and commodities have to be incessantly produced to generate profits. Children were discovered as a niche market in the post–World War II boom in the US – a period which saw a tremendous increase in objects and experiences made "for" children. The process of integrating children into the market as purchasers continued right through the declining real incomes of middle- and working-class people from the '80s onwards. This consumption was now fuelled by debt, which, while it provided new means of realizing capital for the elites (especially the financiers), further enslaved the working class to work – that is, if they could find it. So, we have everyone working harder and longer at more than one job to buy the promises of American capitalism, including a childhood surrounded by playthings.[8]

Marx and Engels had said in 1848 that capital "must nestle everywhere, settle everywhere, establish connections everywhere" ([1848] 2005, 44). Its consequence in our time is the escalating dominance of the market in all social relationships, including our notions of life phases such as youth and childhood. The equation between childhood and consumption, Langer writes, is now hegemonic: "To be a child is to be a consumer of age-specific 'stuff'; to be excluded from consumption is to be denied a 'real childhood'" (2011, 9).

Staging the "Global Generation": The Class Politics of Brand India

Global brands are now ubiquitous in India, perpetuating the hegemonic connection between being a child and having things appropriate to marking one's identity in terms of class, age, gender, sexuality and even politics. Staging their presence through events and performances that may or may not lead to immediate purchases, global brands, nevertheless, do produce identification between privileged childhoods and branded commodities. Disney and AOL-Time Warner characters now make their appearances at cricket matches and malls and in light music and dance shows. In one such performance, Mickey Mouse and Donald Duck danced to popular Bombay cinema songs such as "Just Chill" or "*Dus Bahane*" (Ten Excuses) (Subhajit Banerjee 2006). Disney characters also perform in live shows, as in multiple Indian cities in January 2006 as part of a multi-national campaign in the Asia-Pacific region (Hindu Business Line Bureau 2005).

The advertising blitz necessary to launch these global brands serves to both invent the "global generation" and act as evidence of its existence. Predictably, it is the advertisers and marketers of children's and youth consumer culture who have led the celebratory discourse around the size of the Indian youth market. Suddenly, as if almost overnight, it appears that India's long-lamented high population – with 550 million expected to be under the age of 20 by 2015 – has become an asset.

These figures, however, are widely touted, sometimes with little attention to accuracy. For instance, Shekhar Kapur, a well-known Indian filmmaker who was amongst the first to break into the international market with films such as *Bandit Queen* (1994) and *Elizabeth* (1998), has also recently put his hands in the children's and youth market. Set to produce comic books that both Indianize Western themes, such as Spider-man and Batman, and animate specifically Indian themes.

Kapur called upon children's marketers to "imagine a country with a population of kids twice the size of the entire population of the United States" (Rai 2004, 12).

Referring to the "children of liberalization," Arvind Singhal, chairman of the retail consulting firm KSA Technopak, extolled the virtues of the new generation who, according to him, were "exposed to global trends through TV and the Internet and not [as] spending averse as the previous generation" (Rai 2004, 12). Rohit Bal, India's leading fashion designer who recently launched a children's line, estimated his market of under-14-year-olds at "32 per cent of the one billion residents" (ApunKaChoice Bureau 2004). In a report on BBC, Disney estimated that there were more than 100 million children below 10 years of age (Bajoria 2004). From these accounts, it would appear that *all* Indian children and young people have an equal shot at being consumers.

It is, of course, in the class interest of the professional bourgeoisie – those in advertising, marketing, finance and legal services – to exaggerate both the size of the Indian market and its younger population. The youth factor further exaggerates the size of the market because of the shorter fashion cycle associated with youth or "hipness" or "cool." Furthermore, they position themselves as cultural brokers, inside informants to this large market. As in-betweeners, they play a cultural politics that is simultaneously nationalist and cosmopolitan, pure and hybrid. In his perceptive ethnography of advertising in Mumbai, William Mazzarella (2003) describes, in wonderful detail, the ways in which Indian advertisers stress their insider knowledge of the "uniquely" Indian contexts of consumption – such as the importance of children, weddings or thriftiness – while simultaneously touting the purchasing power of the "world class" Indian consumer to the global brand. Mazzarella argues that flaunting the birth of the Indian "world class" consumer is a means by which the Indian postcolonial bourgeoisie assert their national identity in opposition to (not in compliance with) global capital.

The problem in such a reading is that it takes the nation as the primary category eliding the class divisions within the nation and so takes the class-based rhetoric of the elites at its face value. For, despite their self-representation as harbingers of a "global generation" or the "world class" Indian, marketers are speaking of and to a very specific class-based segment of Indians who can pay for their products. As any marketer knows, the ability to be a consumer depends on one's purchasing power, that is, access to money and commodities. Marketers have no intention of leveling prices or incomes so as to *really* oppose global capital or produce a "global generation." Brokering the entry of multinational capital into India is surely a peculiar way of getting over the humiliations of colonialism!

Consumption in class societies is, as Pierre Bourdieu (1984) elaborated, a means of acquiring "distinction" or a way to establish class hierarchies through the consumption of symbolic and cultural use of capital. Whether this distinction is obtained through foreign, nationalistic or hybrid commodities, it is nevertheless a means of marking separation from others in the nation. Consequently, marketers to children and young people deploy both hybridity and purity to add value to their brands. For their upper-end consumers, marketers advertise and corporations police the "purity" or "authenticity" of foreign brands. Companies, such as Disney, depend on the local legal and police services to protect their brand identity from poaching in a marketplace where small-scale outfits can manufacture exact imitations and disappear without a trace. On my most recent visit to India, the "real" Barbie in an up-scale store in Bombay cost Rs. 600–800. You could easily buy imitations, some called Barbie or Babie for Rs. 50–60. You could also buy pirated Harry Potter or Disney paraphernalia for one-tenth the price of the branded item.

The brand creates distinction amongst otherwise indistinguishable objects and the pirated versions – which ironically, like the branded ones, are mostly made in China – are a source of anxiety for both the marketers and those aspiring to belong to the global bourgeoisie. Prior to the 1980s, the aura of the foreign was maintained in India by state regulation that limited the entry of consumer imports into India. Subsequently, my generation, growing up in the '60s and '70s, will remember the mystique that surrounded the perfumed suitcases of foreign-returned Indians. That very same aura is now maintained by the "free market" which has simply priced the premium foreign brands out of the middle-class market.

In order to reassure and reinforce anxieties about the massification generated by the widespread availability of imitations in India, Sangeeta Talwar, the CEO for Mattel in India, stated in an interview, "We are not into the mass market […] if there is a market for a Ford and a Mercedes Benz there is also a market for Barbie." She followed this with the deal-clincher – an emotional blackmail that measured how much you love your child in terms of how much you are willing to spend on her. "A mother who is worried about her child's health," Talwar continued, "will not want a cheap toy. She'll want the best for her child and that's what we are focusing on" (Bhupta 2001, 4). Advertisements, such as those for Nestle, present smiling images of a mother and a baby with the caption, "I am a no-compromise Mom."

Parents are guilt-tripped into spending money under threat of their children's failure in the competitive academic sphere. Take the following ad for printers, for example. Against the background image of a young boy and girl in school uniforms from whose hands spring forth a series of A+-like butterflies, the copy reads:

HP affordable printing helps your child shine. Printing is now an essential part of education. [...] Now your child can showcase their work at its best.

Labor and Consumption within the Family

The "very best" that a middle-class parent can give her child these days is an education in the English language with an American accent. This is the key to upward mobility secured through a job in the burgeoning information technology or corporate sectors. As the trend towards privatizing higher education has continued, both Indian and global capital have rushed into this lucrative market – with education costs emerging as one of the largest expenses for a middle- to lower-middle-class family. In turn, banks report that, even in the midst of the 2008 economic crisis when credit was declining, education loans continued to increase at the rate of 30–40 percent (Nair and Kumar 2009, 1).

Parents are willing to make extreme sacrifices to acquire an Americanized education for their children. Even middle-class families now send their children abroad for undergraduate education – US leading with UK, Canada, Australia and New Zealand following (Fischer 2010). Schools advertise their global connections, including International Baccalaureate curriculums that are supposed to enable a seamless shift into college in North America, smart-classrooms that are advertised as "future-ready" and global exchanges that supposedly enhance one's competitiveness on a global scale (not foster a sense of citizenship). Topping the bid for a world-class education, the private chain of schools known as The Indian Public School (TIPS), recently bought a school in Los Angeles with plans for Indian students to spend two to three months a year there.

Buying exorbitantly priced foreign brand toys is thus a small part of that larger effort to prepare your child to join the global market. These global toys are seen as a means to acquire the English language and culture and are another variant of the accent schools that have sprung up across India's towns and cities as well as the highly exclusive privatized schools that would match any affluent First World one (J. Kapur 1998). Similarly, the branded toy serves as a lesson in the middle-class work ethic, teaching the child about the necessity of working hard at school to land a high-paying job that would enable purchasing such objects.[9] Higher disposable incomes have not, produced a culture of spending with abandon because of both their recent origins and economic uncertainty. Consequently, despite the encouragement to spend and live in the moment predominant in consumer culture, middle-class consumption is still thrift-centered. Spending on the child is a means to insure the child's future as well as investment in the child's ability to take care of the parent. Although there is a trend, as in the affluent nations, to speak directly to children and invite them to enter the market as consumers, these ads overwhelmingly address parents, stressing upon them the importance of toys as an investment in their child's development.

Spending remains a means to keep one's class position and is thus experienced as work rather than liberation.[10] It is in such a scenario that brands such as McDonalds, Disney and Nickelodeon and Hollywood cultural productions are converted into educational tools. Films such as the *Harry Potter* series become lessons to be mastered – for instance, inter-school quizzes accompanied the films' release in New Delhi. As Aijaz Ahmed (1992, 78) sums it up, "the dominant language of society like the dominant ideology, itself is always the language of the ruling class." In this way toys, Sue Ferguson (2009, 12) surmises, "help shore up the ideological underpinnings essential to the reproduction of specific (national, capitalist) socio-economic, political and cultural relations."

Global Brands and Traditional Hierarchies

There has, however, been a backlash against the consumer culture associated with these global brands in the name of a virulent form of religious fundamentalism and/or nationalism. Its expressions range from public celebrations of nuclear power to reinventing religious rituals in the domestic sphere. Traditional names, audio-video games centered around Hindu myths, big weddings and religious gatherings have become popular with the younger, "hip" set – the same set that also frequents clubs and discos. In part, this is a response to the uncertainties generated by global capital that is mobile and can be withdrawn at any moment – something that is amply visible in the current economic recession. Subsequently, even those professionals who manage to connect to the global system are vulnerable to abrupt withdrawals of investments and a volatile job market. In the last decade and a half, many have gone from unprecedented high salaries to joblessness. Jayati Ghosh and C. P. Chandrashekhar (2002), among others, have confirmed that neoliberalization has brought increased income inequality, which results, as can be expected, in increased pressures on the middle class as it raises the stakes for failure. Religion can offer some comfort in such a situation.

The return to tradition is also pushed by a conservative social agenda in the effort to retain traditional caste, gender and age hierarchies, which are ruptured by the free market. As in the affluent nations, the recognition in India of children and young people as consumers has granted them a certain autonomy and freedom with regards to adult authority and sexual expression. As the cultural historian Gary Cross (1997), recounted, the invention of children as consumers in their own right following World War II in the US was premised upon producing a children's commodity culture that set up an opposition between generations. Driven by the capitalist drive for novelty and planned obsolescence, the toy box, over the course of the twentieth century, became increasingly unrecognizable to parents – a process whose most recent manifestations include video games and content that challenges adult-set social norms. Sexually provocative fashions and toys are then consistent with the logic of commodified youthful rebellion, where each new product line must push the limits of what is socially acceptable.

Commodity Culture and the Battle between Generations

Yet, there is a deeper relation between the sexualization of youth and childhood and the import of novelty in capitalism. "Sex sells" is a mantra that marketers appear to know almost in their bones and deploy it freely, whether in selling cars, clothes or washing machines. Sue Ferguson (2009, 22), brilliantly reading Walter Benjamin, relates the fantastical representations of gender, sexuality and violence of so many commoditoys to the culture of capitalism. She works with two of Benjamin's significant insights into capitalism. The first was that the incessant display of commodities, each rapidly giving way to the next, upheld the mythic belief in capitalism as a system that promised abundance, change and a better future. It led to a belief in the market as the source of solutions to all problems. The second was that an obsession with death was particularly embedded in commodity culture – both in general and in fashion. Since commodity culture is driven by novelty and the truly novel experience is death, David McNally (2001, 203) reads Benjamin to suggest that commodity culture relentlessly "moves ever closer to death." It is "in keeping with this logic," Ferguson explains, that "those toys, games and media that can be interpreted as brushing up against mortality are such strong sellers" (2009, 25). And there has been without doubt an escalation in explorations of death in children's and youths' consumer culture.

The other connection that Benjamin traced between death and commodity culture went back to Marx's theory of alienation – that, in the marketplace, power is invested in things rather than in the people who make those things, thus producing a trance-like existence in which dead objects, including money, are worshipped. Fashion dolls are, Ferguson explains, in this sense another twist on necrophilia in so far as they invite the human to conform to the impossible standards set in plastic and, so in "represent[ing] the body's coupling with the inorganic, they introduce the erotic powers of death and decay into the very fibres of children's culture" (2009, 26). In other words, death is itself eroticized and the thrill of a brush with death is amongst the most riveting of sales pitches. The fundamental subversiveness of sexuality, its conscious and subconscious refusal to be bound up within social norms, also makes it a powerful hook for the thrill of novelty and risk that drives commodity culture.

The promise of an adrenaline rush may be easily observed in children's war games and is a well-worn cliché in the car marketing aimed at young people. Take for instance, the following car advertisement, which is part of a rampant sales pitch for cars as the Indian market has opened up to global manufacturers. The young and upcoming cricketer, Virat Kohli, is shown in three images. At the top – eyes closed arms wide open – he is shown ready to jump off a cliff while secured to a parked car by a rope – how the car got to the end of the cliff, we don't know! Below it in the second picture, we see Kohli flying down the cliff, and, in the third image, he is scoring a run on the cricket pitch, helmet in hand. The copy reads:

> You know adrenaline is on the move
> When it courses through your veins
> Like a runaway train.
> When it makes your heart pound
> In anticipation and your mouth
> Open in a silent scream of delight.
> A feeling so powerful, we call it waku-doki
> Or what you feel when you drive a Fortuner.

Although the sexualization of public space through commodity culture remains tied to selling commodities, it has, nevertheless, fostered a moral panic and a reaction. Taking recourse to religious fundamentalism, reactionary groups enact the strange paradox of wanting capitalism without capitalism, that is, without its challenges to the social conventions of caste, gender and age. For instance, the Shiv Sena, a Hindu fundamentalist party, sees no contradiction between banning Valentine's Day as a Western entity and buying off the land of the striking textile mill, Kohinoor Mills, and turning it into a mall. In its party paper, *Saamna*, it frequently invokes a vituperative masculinity as response to the sexualization of consumer culture. In the following excerpt, rape is justified as the direct result of consumer culture:

> In the name of remixes, the wave of 'sex-appeal' is ruining entire generations.
> If an adolescent boy develops perverse tendencies because of such hot movies

and their obscene posters, and an innocent girl falls victim to that, then who is to blame? The boy's perversity or society? (Saamna 2005)

This kind of moral panic used to justify patriarchal policing is not limited to the fundamentalist political parties alone, but widespread as a middle-class phenomenon. For instance, an inter-religious organization, the Federation of Culture Upgradation and Social Services (FOCUSS), was formed in Hyderabad in 2005 with the express purpose to "wage a campaign against petting and kissing in public places, especially parks" (Radhakrishna 2005). Indian television serials are filled with family dramas that revolve around the preservation of patriarchal tradition via the celebration of religious ritual.

In such a situation, hybridity, or the mixing up of cultures, appears subversive and is celebrated as such by those who give primacy to culture.[11] Furthermore, it is not just the elites who are hybridizing culture. Imitations, such as blond, blue-eyed dolls that dance to popular Hindi film music or pirated Mickey Mouse logos on children's goods ranging from steel spoons to t-shirts, are available at the lower end of the market. Culture is not an alienable commodity and consumers give it their own interpretation and agency, despite the efforts of corporations to limit it to their brand identities – a phenomenon Cultural Studies has drawn so much attention to. A few years ago, I found the Nike "Swoosh" logo quite popular among cab drivers in Bombay who would draw it on the trunks or bumpers of their taxis. However, they did not simply reproduce it and the sign was sometimes inverted, doubled, or even tripled. When I asked what the symbol actually meant, not one identified it as Nike – I was told that it was a hockey stick. Perhaps, the Nike "Swoosh" was seen as a hockey stick or interpreted as one – either way, the point is that it was not identified with Nike products and used instead as a nice decoration in keeping with one of India's popular sport obsessions.

Ultimately, though, this discussion on hybridity does not go beyond mere descriptions or celebrations of agency. To look for resistance to capital in hybridity is to forget that hybridity is written into the capitalist production of culture itself and stems from its drive for novelty. In terms of economic logic, novelty is necessary to find new markets as well as beat competition. In terms of culture, novelty is the premise upon which capitalism presents itself as a system that generates abundance, choice and incessant improvement. Driven to produce new commodities and markets, capital constantly cannibalizes cultural forms transforming them into commodities. It is this tendency that has brought us the likes of Maharaja Mac and "ethnic chic."

Consumption in capitalist societies is ultimately a feature of class stratification and individuation. Envy, or "aspiration" as the advertisers prefer to say, is its driving emotion as well as the glue that attaches people to the system. Fashion poaches on subaltern cultures for ideas, turning them into expensive high fashion commodities. Take, for instance, the practice of tattooing. Initially, a working-class aesthetic practice, it is now embraced as a fun expression by elites, both in the US and India, turning it into an expensive form of adornment. As the practice becomes popular, it will also soon become passé. Because the system feeds on class anxieties, newer commodities will have to be produced to mark distinction and the cycle continues.

While such cycling of commodities produces a certain surface leveling of consumption (working class use of blue jeans and mobile phones are cited as instances of the trickle-down benefits of neoliberalism in India) it is not to be mistaken with a leveling of opportunities or resources. There is nothing systemically subversive, for example, about the Indian elite who, like their postmodern counterparts from the affluent world, consume what was previously considered kitsch – such as popular Hindi cinema or a mish-mash of the local and global – ironically and self-reflexively.

My research corroborates Leela Fernandes' (2006) conclusions that hybridity in contemporary urban India is inextricably linked to the class-based cosmopolitanism Indian-ness of the urban middle classes. This cosmopolitanism, expressed primarily through the consumption of global and Indian brands, is a means of secession from the nation paradoxically represented as an assertion of Indian-ness. The paradox works because nationalism itself is being redefined as consumption by a state whose primary function has become to smooth the entry of global capital into the country.

Shopping is a Patriotic Duty

It is in Brand India that "world class" Indian consumers do India proud and can shed their previous, even if hypocritical, visage of embarrassment around consumption and turn it into a nationalist duty. For instance, India's Independence Day, 15 August, is now an occasion for sales. Biba, a fashion house, announced a "flat 40% off" sale and Honda a "freedom offer" discount on a car. Emblematic of this change in attitude is the following excerpt from an interview with Sheetal Mafatlal, a member of one of India's foremost capitalist families, who has bought international brands, such as the designer fashion label Valentino, into the Indian market.

Do you think mindsets have to be addressed? Do you think people feel guilty about seeming to be spending on luxury goods in a country like India?
    I think India is changing – it reflects in the food we eat, the way people dress, in the restaurant boom, in the media.

Do you feel that you represent the new Indian spender?
      You have to do what you have to do without making any apologies for it.
(Gahlaut 2007)

This refusal to apologize for conspicuous consumption is the sign of a fundamental break; it is ultimately a disavowal of shared citizenship. Pitching unapologetic self-centeredness as an aspirational ideal, an advertisement for housing puts these words in the mouth of its silhouetted subject: "I like my views just like my diamonds. Bigger and better than everyone else's." You will be able to succeed, the ad appears to say, by literally moving upwards into these "sky villas" whose "double-height views" make "the world outside look twice as nice."[12] Those living below these heights are now only an image, a view.

      Yet, for all the celebration of the dawning of the age of the Indian consumer, the typical Indian consumer is already consuming far less than their needs and India has the dubious distinction of having the largest amount of child labor in the world with sixty million working in conditions akin to slavery by a 1998 International Labour Organization (ILO) estimate. For Brand India this is no more than a PR problem that tarnishes its image. When the story of children working in horrendous conditions in a Delhi sweatshop producing for the clothing company Gap broke, the Indian minister of commerce, Kamal Nath, chastised nongovernmental organizations (NGOs) for bringing "bad publicity" which, he argued, would lead to barriers against products imported from India. In other words, such information would destroy the competitive edge India enjoys because of its worker's poverty and that compelled children into labor akin to conditions of slavery (David 2007). The very same arguments in support of child labor were made by British capitalists in the late nineteenth century who argued that children's labor increased the profitability of British manufacturing.[13]

      While those who champion liberalization, such as Jagdish Bhagwati (2004), claim that there has been a decline in the percentage of those living under the poverty line, others verify that India, over the last decade of the twentieth century, has sharply polarized into "Two Indias." This is the title of a write-up by Randeep Ramesh (2006) on the gulfs that separate the First World lifestyles of the few – in gated communities governed by their private schools, hospitals, roads and police – and the majority – living in a reality characterized by P. Sainath (2009) as the "Indianization of income and globalization of prices." As evidence, Sainath cites India's fall from number 127 to 132 out of 159 nations on the United Nations Human Development Index (HDI) in 2009. This means that the much-celebrated, huge market exists in a nation where the majority of the people are amongst the poorest in the world – coming shockingly behind even Palestine and Botswana.

For the middle class, squeezed between these two polarities, a high investment in their children's education is the only safeguard against an increasingly volatile economy. As Barbara Ehrenreich (1990) explains in her study of the US middle class, the only way the middle class can ensure that their children remain in their ranks is by educating them so that they can enter professions as adults. At the same time, it is in its class' interest to jealously guard these professions by setting up elaborate sets of rules and extended training periods. Obviously, these pressures increase when the size of the middle class shrinks.

The Labor of Childhood

Facing these increased pressures, middle-class children race against each other – taking coaching classes as early as four years of age to prepare for the impending interview to enter a coveted kindergarten. This deadly competition is encouraged by media reports of children achieving academic landmarks at unbelievably young ages. For instance, Aditya Patil was a Microsoft-certified systems engineer by age 11 and offered a job by the Bill Gates Corporation (Mascarenhas 2004). Sushma Verma, a seven-year-old, successfully completed the tenth grade, beating Tathagat Avatar Tulsi who had done this feat earlier at the age of nine (*Indian Express* 2007b). The flip side of these grueling pressures are the hoaxes, such as that played by a 15-year-old who claimed that he had topped a NASA exam and earned an interview with the then president of India, Abul Kalam (Kaushik 2005).

Youth for Sale

Contrary to the claims of the children's marketers, India's "global generation" is being integrated into global capital primarily as labor and not as consumers, with intellectual labor in the burgeoning service and IT industry as a top career choice. A core commodity of Brand India, as its site boasts, is a large English-educated, technically proficient labor force that promises to reduce labor costs and add value. Its added advantage, according to Jairam Ramesh, member of the Indian parliament, Rajya Sabha (Congress I), is that it operates in a time zone advantageous in relation to the US; "You are working when America is sleeping, and when America is working, you are still working!" (J. Ramesh 2005).

India as a whole – despite its 55 billionaires, housing some of the richest men in the world and a minority group of transnational bourgeoisie – remains peripheral to the global economy and a source for capitalist accumulation for the Global North. It is precisely this center-periphery relationship that enabled the Global North, following World War II, to transition into a consumer economy by shifting production to the Third World – a process radicalized at the end of the twentieth century through credit, new technologies and business practices that made it possible for capital to decentralize production while centralizing profits.

In showing the continued relevance of imperialism as a defining feature of the current phase of capitalist expansion, William Tabb (2007) explains that capitalism is inherently a global system. It is driven outwards *not* by the demands and needs of the consumer but by the drive to generate more capital via new markets, cheap labor and technological innovation. In other words, Barbie's entry into India is a means for generating profits for Mattel and not a response to the needs and demands of Indian children. Ultimately, the core commodity of Brand India is its young people – both as a market and as labor. While the former cultivates the image of childhood and youth as a time of freedom and spontaneity, the latter relentlessly turns the same period into training for or direct involvement in the global labor force. The purchasing power of the former is vastly exaggerated while, in reality, childhood for the overwhelming majority is either a time for labor or preparation for it. What does this mean for the relationship between the old and the young?

Capitalism and the Politics of Generations

In recent year, there has been a resurgence of interest in the sociology of generations. June Edmunds and Bryan S. Turner (2005) recount that, beginning in the second half of the twentieth century, the earlier concept of a generation as a cohort defined according to chronological age was replaced by Mannheim's (1997) concept of generation as a cohort constituted by history. Mannheim claimed that a generation is constructed as a cohort through some shared traumatic historical experience; for example, World War I marked the generation of the 1920s generation or Vietnam that of the '60s.

Mannheim attributed the emergence of generations to the fast-paced change in modernization that deepened the gap between the past and the future, making what the old knew increasingly irrelevant in the present. Edmunds and Turner, expanding on Mannheim, suggested that such historical moments were global in nature and so proposed the term "global generation." According to them, the 1960s saw the birth of the first "global generation" united by new media technologies, social and political movements and a certain degree of economic security. Leena Alanen (1994) has introduced the concept of "generationing" (an idea akin to gendering) to conceptualize the process by which identities based in age are produced. Accordingly, the production of a so-called "global generation," or a global teenager or child, through marketing efforts may be seen as a "generationing" process – one that produces young people who identify with a cohort across national boundaries.

The concept of generations and its grounding in history is helpful in that it foregrounds the changing nature of relationships between the old and the young and tries to grapple with the experience of time itself over the course of the twentieth century and into our own. The problem, however, is that it takes the notion of a generation as a primary category, delinking it from historical modes of production. In what is basically a liberal – as opposed to a historical – materialist view, historical change is presented as an outcome of a clash between generations rather than between social relations of production.

In this approach, there is no way to consider how the very nature of childhood or adulthood is, itself, socially constructed in historical contexts. For instance, the discovery and marketing of youth as a commodity – an attitude or lifestyle since the 1960s – has dispersed youth widely in society, driving it both up and down the age span. Children are integrated as savvy consumers while the market offers adults and older people the promise of an eternal youth. In other words, consumer culture has incessantly blurred the boundaries between the young and the old – a process that has really accelerated in the last decades of the twentieth century and into the twenty-first.[14] As, Heinz Hengst (2005, 36) concludes, commodification and the assertion of consumer culture that characterizes contemporary globalization "comes to children without passing the 'generation' filter."

At the same time, the disciplinary regime of capital has increasingly colonized both childhood and old age, expanding the time given up to alienated labor both up and down in the life span. At the heart of the war between labor and capital, is the latter's incessant drive to lower the costs of social reproduction and to privatize those costs by passing them off to families and individuals. Now, as capital has become ever more mobile and its access to a global labor force magnified, it has become even freer to absolve itself of investing in social reproduction. After all, you can simply move your investment to another cheaper source of labor – both geographically and in terms of chronological age. All across the globe, then – including Europe with its historically more progressive provisions of social welfare – we are witnessing the withdrawal of social welfare and the unbearable stresses it places on the family and individuals. In India, we have children either directly laboring to sustain the global economy or training hard in preparation for it, while the hard won concept of retirement with security and dignity is quickly fading away as a distant fantasy.

In designating the 1960s as the first "global generation," primarily because of the connections made possible by communication technologies, Edmunds and Turner neglect the sense of internationalism that was at the core of socialism. As capitalism integrated the world it also produced an international response against it and the militant call, "workers of all countries unite," was, if nothing else, entirely global in its ambition. Moreover, the tendency to regard the clash between generations as both inevitable and creative echoes the drama of generations staged by a fashion-dictated consumer culture that relentlessly presents the new as a rebellion against the old and celebrates novelty for its own sake. To use this oedipal motif in place of class struggle as the engine of change is to deny the significance of history, memory and intergenerational solidarity in working-class life.

The struggles between generations, Pierre Bourdieu (1993) clarifies, have invariably unfolded against historically specific distributions of resources and the chances of obtaining them. What is unfolding before us, I think, is a tightening of the capitalist noose around the possibilities of the human life, our ability to learn and unlearn constantly and desire for harmony rather than antagonism between generations. Capitalism has certainly, through its deployment of youth as the engine that animates the fashion cycles of commodity culture, extended youth and given us a glimmer of what a post-generation world may look like. Yet, it limits that promise to individual purchasing power, while simultaneously proletarianizing on a global scale both childhood and old age. As one generation replaces another in the market, human life at its two ends appears a burden. The individual disconnected from the market joins the ranks of the "surplus" population. It is in the midst of this impoverishment of human life as a whole that the obsession with youth in capitalist commodity culture appears sickeningly desperate and tacky.

The celebratory discourse around youth consumer culture in India would have us believe that this is India's first "global generation." But this is not so. There is still a generation alive – now grandmothers and grandfathers – who were born in colonial India and came of age in that first wave of exploitation by global capital. In order to sell India once again to global capital, its leaders have to empty the nation of its people and their troublesome historical memories, such as the following trenchant reminder by Randhir Singh:

> Before 1947, we were part of a global system, well-integrated into a world market economy. We were globalized, so to speak, but we did not like it. Our globalization, then also had a name, imperialism, and we struggled against it, precisely because its structural logic meant the accumulation of wealth in England and poverty in India. Like other Third World countries, we wanted to get out of this globalization to be able to opt for an independent, self-reliant development in the interests of our common people.

[…] Now India is being globalized again this time through a largely voluntary submission of India's rulers who are opting out to be junior partners to the global capitalist system. The national project finally and definitively collapsed in 1991. (1999, 32–3)

At the same time, as we learn from Marx, capitalism carries within it the seeds of its own destruction – the integration of the young into capital is also turning them against it. This is evident in a schoolchildren's protest in India for textbooks and against Coca-Cola and PepsiCo for the high levels of pesticides in their drinks (BBC News 2005), teenage Chinese workers who documented their conditions of work and went on strike (Perry 2007) and the militant anti-capitalism of the anti-globalization movements since Seattle in 1999 that re-emerged with new vigor following the 2008 crisis. Now that is a "global generation" which Brand India dare not celebrate!

Individualist preoccupations with the future of one's own children and aspirations for upward mobility or escape through the consumption of global brands may well keep the middle class tethered to neoliberalism. But, two decades of neoliberal restructuring, the narrowing of choices for children and the escalating high stakes for "making it" in the current economy could well loosen the strings. It could once again bring the generations together against capital.

Chapter 2

ARRESTED DEVELOPMENT AND THE MAKING OF A NEOLIBERAL STATE

In *Shishu* (Children), a short story by Mahasweta Devi ([1978] 1993), a junior government officer, Singh, is sent to distribute relief to the underdeveloped areas along India's eastern border. Perplexed by the regular theft of government supplies from his camp, Singh keeps watch and one night comes upon a group of children running towards the forest with their loot. He sets after them, finally catching up at the boundary where the government camp ends and the forest begins. The children now turn around and start to close upon him in a circle. It is then, that he realizes – in stunned shock and disbelief – that they are not children but adults – old men and women with grey hair, weathered breasts and penises. Describing the encounter, Devi (250–51) writes:

> They cackled with savage and revengeful glee. Cackling, they ran around him. They rubbed their organs against him and told him that they were adult citizens of India. […] They cackled in the vicious joy born out of desire for revenge.
>
> […] But revenge against what?
>
> Singh's shadow covered their bodies. And that shadow brought the realization home to him. They hated his height of five feet and nine inches. They hated the normal growth of his body. His normalcy was the crime they could not forgive.
>
> Singh's cerebral cells tried to register the logical explanation but he failed to utter a single word. Why, why this revenge? He did not have the stature of a healthy Russian, Canadian or an American. He did not eat food that supplied enough calories for a human body. The World Health Organization said that it was a crime to deny the human body of the right number of calories.
>
> But he could not utter a single word in his own defense. Standing still under the moon, listening to their deafening voices, shivering at the rubbing of their organs against his body, Singh knew that the ill-nourished and ridiculous body of an ordinary Indian was the worst crime in the history of civilization.

It was through the searing image of the shrunken "adult citizens of India" that Mahashweta Devi taunted and prodded the paternalistic *mai-baap*[1] demeanor of the so-called development state. Yet, she also ended with the representative of the same state – the middle-class, urban, low-ranking bureaucrat Singh – recoiling in paralyzing shame and anguish from the failures of such a state. For in the final analysis, Singh's revulsion stemmed from a fundamental principle of the development state and its origins in the anti-colonial movement. It was the notion that the nation, won collectively through struggle, places upon the postcolonial nation state a moral imperative to redress long-standing inequities with justice. After all, how else could the postcolonial state differentiate itself from the colonial rulers? And it was upon this foundation of postcolonial citizenship that Devi's "adult citizens of India" indicted the nation for its sick and bankrupt arrested development.

The shift to neoliberalism has entailed a clear break from this sense of collective responsibility and replaced it, instead with the radical individualism of an atomistic, amoral subject – a subject who conceives of the self as a commodity to be packaged, bought, and sold on the market and in completion with others. Such a subject, I will argue, experiences life increasingly as beholden to fate and is fascinated by and drawn to authoritarian, fascist projects as a resolution to existential anxieties born out of a sense of personal insignificance and meaninglessness. The perception that life is an accident of fate runs through capitalism and unites both elites and the dispossessed. While the nature and quality of this perception varies according to class, it nevertheless offers the religious Right an undercurrent to draw upon and offers a way to address existential anxieties without touching its structural inequalities. For instance, the current popularity and revival of ancient Hindu texts among business elites echoes quite nicely with neoliberal tenets of individualism and the demand for a so-called non-interventionist state – that is, non-interventionist so far as imposing any restraints on capital is concerned. Stated differently, there is nothing innately Indian about the appeal of religiosity, as some strands of postmodern and postcolonial theory would suggest, but rather it is a timely response to contemporary reality.[2]

To get back to Devi's story, written in the late '70s, *Shishu* should serve as a rejoinder to those who continue to describe the preliberalization state as socialistic. Far from it, the postcolonial state immediately following independence is best described, as Randhir Singh does, as a form of statist-capitalism that thrived on and profited from uneven development in the country. Its protectionism and trade barriers, also known as "Nehruvian socialism," essentially supported military spending and industrial development in favor of the national bourgeoisie. As Perry Anderson recounts, under Nehru no land reforms were enacted, income tax was not introduced until 1961 and primary education was grossly neglected.[3] Dominated by rich farmers, urban professionals and traders, the Congress Party kept intact the pattern of uneven development – pockets of wealth in the midst of poverty – characteristic of capitalism.

By the late '70s, in the period that formed the background of Devi's story, monopoly houses such as the Birlas and Tatas were well ensconced and there was a sizeable middle class as well as a nouveau-rich agrarian class borne of the Green Revolution. Meanwhile, gross inequalities marked both the rural and urban landscape, leading to widespread social and labor unrest. Indira Gandhi, the then prime minister, attempted to repress these various agitations by declaring a state of Emergency in 1975 that lasted for nineteen months. During this period, all civil rights and liberties were frozen and prisons filled with anyone suspected of political opposition. Randhir Singh (2010) reminding us of this history, points out that to describe the postcolonial state as socialistic not only denies the class project of the national bourgeoisie but also serves the ideological function of presenting neoliberalism as a break from the failures of socialism rather than as an even greater dose of uneven development already in place under statist-capitalism. He writes:

> Its [the state's] rhetoric of 'a socialistic pattern of society' only deceived the people and […] created confusion about it as 'socialism' that persists to this day; it is the failure of this capitalism to deliver that continues to be misinterpreted as the failure of socialism in India. (34)

Correcting the cliché that Nehru had a "vision of socialism," Randhir Singh (1999) sarcastically rejoined that Nehru had, in fact, reduced socialism to a vision. That vision lay then, as it does now, with people's movements that have tried to put brakes on the private accumulation of wealth.

The naked, shriveled adults of Devi's story, then, were an indictment of the façade of the socialist rhetoric of the development state, or its refusal to live up to the adulthood of a self-reliant nation committed to social justice for its citizens. This denunciation could only be premised upon a notion of the state as an embodiment of people's struggles for equity and justice.[4] In creating a character like Singh, Devi put her finger on the self-loathing that urban middle- and upper-middle-class Indians may, in some honest moment, encounter when confronted with the stark, humiliating poverty that surrounds us. In fact, she holds up this ability to experience a shared notion of citizenship as a mark of human integrity and depth taking us through the stages of middle-class comprehension in three pithy stages at the end of the story.

Confronted by the withered adulthood of his fellow citizens, Devi's Singh first responds with self-pity and immediately compares himself with the citizens of the First World. But once he moves past that and recognizes those who surround and mock him as fellow citizens, the bottom appears to fall out.

Yet, he does not descend into madness and fear. Instead, tears of shame and grief roll down his eyes. Devi writes:

> The only recourse left to Singh was to go stark, raving mad, tearing his expanse apart with the a howl like that of a mad dog. But why wasn't his brain ordering his vocal chords to scream and scream and scream? Only tears ran down his cheeks. ([1987] 1993, 251)

Thus, Singh comes into a burning awareness of his own complicity in a system whose "relief" is better stolen than received gratefully. In fact, the premise of Devi's condemnation is that it is the state that robs the tribal inhabitants, laying claims to their forests and minerals and driving them further into the receding forest. What it means to be further integrated into such a state is already well known to the latter. It is to turn into disposable labor in a perpetual state of migration – in domestic work, farms, mines and other innumerable changeable jobs, whether closer to home or in India's urban centers. The bitter irony of receiving charity from the thief who steals your wealth is not lost on the shriveled adults who circle Singh, jabbing him with their age and history – both emblematic of a deeper knowledge.

The Neoliberal State and the Rise of the Economic Individual

The shift to neoliberalism has been marked by a momentum to pry open the notion of citizenship from its roots in the history of the innumerable sacrifices, struggles and hopes that won India its freedom from the British Empire. It was this history that gave the postcolonial state the moral imperative, even if largely rhetorical, to secure equity and distributive justice within a program of economic growth that aimed towards self-reliance. The Nehruvian state born of this history did have some achievements to its credit, in particular, a secure middle class that formed the basis of its liberal democracy, a public sector in health, higher education, transport and electricity and a certain commitment to democratic principles underlying institutions such as an independent judiciary. But the most significant legacy of the anti-colonial movement lay in the expectation that the state should act on behalf of the majority of its electorate. It is a legacy that continues to act as a restrain on the shift to neoliberalism. It is the moral charge that animates protests against Special Economic Zones (SEZs) and the depletion of natural resources via corporate take-over of land and water – as in the ouster of Vedanta mining from Orissa or the Tatas from Bengal.

Nevertheless, the year 1991, as Randhir Singh (2010) remarked, signaled the final and irrevocable break of the Indian bourgeoisie from the nationalist project. Claiming to shoot out of history and enter the world stage as a global power, neoliberalism raises the economy as an autonomous sphere disconnected from politics, presents a world-view in which action must necessarily occur in a morally ambiguous world, and, ultimately, validates a nihilistic subject for whom the past and the future have unraveled, leaving in its place a sense of time in which the present incessantly dissolves into nothingness.

The Making of a Neoliberal State: A Brief Outline

Beginning in the middle of the 1980s, the Indian state started to open the country to global capital under the then prime minister, Rajiv Gandhi. Gandhi cast himself as a new phenomenon on the political scene – as someone who would break the shackles of the previous restraint on free enterprise and consumption described as "Nehruvian socialism" and advocated for by his grandfather, Nehru. One of Gandhi's preferred slogans – which proclaimed his break (versus continuity) with history – was that he was going to take India into the twenty-first century.[5]

The three pillars of Rajiv Gandhi's so-called "break" from this history of "socialist" constraints on free enterprise were: one, an emphasis on technology and experts as a solution to poverty and underdevelopment; two, removing the restrictions on capital as a way of "liberating" free enterprise; three, celebrating an ethos of spending for a middle class ready to shed its coyness around consumption inherited from the anti-colonial struggle. Under Rajiv Gandhi, import and export restrictions on capital were loosened and Indian capital's collaboration with foreign capital made easier. Rajeev Gandhi's favored project, the Maruti car – an Indo-Italian collaboration that opened up the Indian auto market – was born at this conjuncture. The Indian market was also opened to the import of both capital and consumer goods. Then in 1991, under the supervision of the International Monetary Fund (IMF) and the World Bank, the Indian state formally initiated the program of structural adjustment which had all the features of neoliberalism: privatization and de-regulation of publicly held assets, erosion of labor laws in favor of capital, greater degree of financialization and a firm belief in the free market.

As the brief outline above indicates, the postcolonial state has consistently regulated the labor-capital relationship in favor of the latter. It has taken this to a new level in steering the shift towards neoliberalism. Firstly, as Pratyush Chandra and Dipankar Basu (2007) have indicated, the neoliberal state intervenes on behalf of capital to secure control over resources – both natural and human – and, secondly, it disguises this role by insisting on an ideological separation between the political and the economic, thus safeguarding capital against the political interventions of labor and the dispossessed. The exclusion of the political from the economic has been, from the seventeenth century of John Locke and onwards, a core tenet of liberal social theory. This separation underpins the notion that the "free market" is an autonomous economic sphere with its own self-correcting mechanisms. Marx corrected this, showing the integral interconnection between the economic and the political. He explained that far from being "free" the market was a mechanism of labor exploitation and, therefore, inseparable from politics – that is, the struggle over resources. Labor, unless organized, would perpetually be at the losing end of the free market.

Now, in its most recent restoration as neoliberalism, free market ideology is deployed to justify dismantling the development functions of the postcolonial state. It divests the postcolonial state of its conception as a buffer (if not an activist advocate) between capital and its most marginalized citizens. The task of "relief" is now outsourced to nongovernmental organizations (NGOs), whose guiding principle is a bland professionalism that replaces the notion of redistributive justice that may be expected from the representatives of a democratic state. The sheer abyss of shame experienced by the development worker in Mahasweta Devi's story would, in this new incarnation, be an old-fashioned relic from another time when the self was implicated in the poverty of others in the nation.

At War, Within and Without: The Bourgeois Subject of Neoliberalism

Large political economic changes such as the redefinition of citizenship do not occur in a vacuum, but are rehearsed and contested in culture. And, it is in culture that we can read the nature of the bourgeois subject of the neoliberal project. In the midst of a dismissal of the recent past (that is, the notion that India has broken out of its colonial past to emerge as a brand-new global power) we may discern a new-found enthusiasm amongst the neoliberal *avant-garde* – the marketers, the executives and the leading capitalists – for an even older, more ancient past, that is, the *Mahabharata*.[6] In particular, there is great enthusiasm around interpreting the *Gita*, which contains Krishna's teaching to Arjuna in the battle-field urging him not only to defeat, but to annihilate his brothers who are now his enemies. Krishna moves Arjuna to overcome his resistance to killing his own brothers by advising him to adopt the stance of a *karmayogi*, that is, to achieve the unity of mind and body with the universe through action.[7] He advises Arjuna to perform his *karma*, which, according to the caste-bound, patriarchal set of duties known as *Dharma*, enjoins Arjuna (who is *Kshatriya*, of the warrior caste) to go to war. The essence of Krishna's teaching, as distilled in the common-place understanding of *karmayoga*, is to do one's duty without any attachment to or expectation for results.

Management gurus now cite the *Mahabharata* as the primary source of lessons for living in and maneuvering the bylanes and highways of the new business environment – an environment now seen as inseparable from life itself. It is not my intention to get into a debate about the correct interpretation of the *Gita* because to do so is to accept the premise that religion is an autonomous entity significant for its own sake and so must be answered in its own terms, that is, through interpretation of religious texts. Since these religious texts are being reinterpreted for living in the present, it is to the political uses of these interpretations in the present that we must turn to as a doorway to understanding how the political project of the religious Right resonates with neoliberalism.

Leading in the corpus of management self-help books based on the *Mahabharata* are Debashis Chatterjee's *Timeless Leadership: 18 leadership Sutras from the Bhagavad Gita* (2012) and Gurcharan Das' *The Difficulty of Being Good: On the Subtle Art of Dharma* (2009). Chatterjee has also designed a course for business executives around the *Mahabharta* and the *Gita* and offers it in business schools, including the Harvard Business School. Both Das and Chatterjee's books are endorsed by leading figures in MBA education. The *karmayoga* concept is popular in the industry as well. A paid advertisement that appeared in all national dailies marking the death anniversary of Dhirubhai Ambani, India's leading capitalist and amongst the top-five wealthiest men in the world, hailed Ambani as a *karmayogi* and went on quote the *Mahabharata*: "With determination and command over the senses, a true *karmayogi* embarks on the right path of action."

The notable fact about the contemporary revival of the *Mahabharata* by the management gurus is that they present their readings as a way to cope with a new situation, not simply as a return to tradition. Indeed, in one way this tack is completely in synch with the *Hindutva* claim that Hinduism is a monolith that, in the ancient past, discovered everything that has to be discovered and its insights remain just as relevant today. So if, as the *Hindutva* narrative goes, the ancient Hindus discovered planes, nuclear energy and cosmetic surgery hundreds of years ago, what is to stop them from discovering the principles of making it in the turbulent seas of financial capital in the twenty-first century? There is no denying that there is a certain twinge of pride and self-interest with which Indian business literature, overwhelmingly produced by the upper castes who are also quite prominent in business education in the US, claims an innate superiority in the knowledge of capitalism, particularly at a time when US foreign policy sees India as an ally and economic power that can balance China.[8]

Yet, to explain the contemporary revival of the *Mahabharata* as a bid by the Hindu bourgeoisie to assert *Hindutva* pride is to touch the most obvious level of explanation. In fact, Das, anticipating this line of criticism, takes pains to elaborate that he read the *Mahabharata* not as a religious text but as a cultural one appropriate for our times. Indeed, in order to see how the *Hindutva* project converges with the neoliberal project, we must move beyond religion and read these interpretations for the insights they offer into the making of neoliberal subjectivities.

It is significant that both Das and Chatterjee offer their readings of the *Mahabharata* to the well-heeled, cosmopolitan and educated middle to upper-middle class. In keeping with the particular category of the self-help genre that merges lessons from management with how to live, these readings are meant to offer individualistic solutions to existential crises as well as serve as guides for success in business and the corporate ladder; that is, they preach approaching life itself as an entrepreneurial enterprise now raised to the level of spiritual practice.[9] For instance, Gurcharan Das (2009) offers his personal reasons for turning to the *Mahabharta* after a successful thirty-year climb up the corporate hierarchy, during which he had worked with some of the most prestigious multinational firms in India, as follows:

> How long could an adult be expected to be motivated by a 0.5% gain in the monthly market shares of Vicks Vaporub or Pampers? I felt weary by the time I was fifty, and it was this feeling of futility, that drove me, in part to early retirement. (xiv)

The conclusions he arrives at about the meaning of life are, however, entirely compatible with spending a lifetime generating profits for the corporate machine. Life, Das tells us, "[…] may well be absurd and futile" (xiv). Chatterjee (2012), too, finds confirmation in the *Mahabharata* about the stresses of life on the corporate ladder and goes on to enumerate Arjuna's "symptoms" as "[…] all-too-familiar to us in our own stressful times: grief, loss of meaning, and inability to carry the burden of mounting performance pressures" (199). In another section, he equates Arjuna's inability to act with those "sore points of inaction and indecision […] that require the CEO to go through major emotional upheavals such as life-style changes [read downsizing], turnaround plans [read outsourcing to competition], confronting nonperformance, or bringing negative news to the organization [read job loss, business closure]" (34).

Both writers speak of the marketplace as a war zone, turning the *Mahabharata* into a how-to manual for contemporary corporate soldiers. As Chatterjee explains:

> The unpredictability of the battle for the marketshare and mindshare, the volatility of the environment, and the rapid-fire changes that are happening in the business and political landscape have all the trappings of a full-scale war. (2)

The central lesson of the *Mahabharta*, Das summarizes, is to live according to this principle: "adopt a friendly face to the world but do not allow yourself to be exploited" (2009, xlvii). In this reading, the *Mahabharata* has been updated to speak the tenets of free market theory that everyone must first and foremost calculate his or her own self-interest and everyone is equally open to being exploited by others. The way to cope with the unpredictable ups and downs of the market, according to both Das and Chatterjee, requires a certain detachment regarding outcomes – a detachment born of the knowledge that the outcome is out of control of the individual capitalist and an acceptance of the meaninglessness of this worldly life.

Das goes so far as to say that guardedness and disinterest – necessary attributes in a state of war – must extend to one's family and children as well. Taking the example of B. Ramalinga Raju, the owner-founder of the IT company Satyam, whose fraudulent account-keeping led to what is called the "Indian Enron" scandal, Das explains that Raju was ruined by a "weakness for his sons," that is, his desire to leave each of his sons a company (278).

> The *Mahabharta* seems to be saying that one ought to nurture one's children, but one does not have to indulge them […] nor leave them with a company each. […] it takes moral courage to resist the partiality towards one's family [… and] behave with impartiality towards everyone. (278–9)

Raju manipulated the company's accounts to show profits that were non-existent, thus keeping the company afloat in the stock market. When the fraud came to light, he was not able to pay his shareholders and the company went bankrupt, taking with it the savings of those who had invested in its stocks. According to Das, this was a calculated gamble on Raju's part and not an immoral choice. After all, Das elaborated, if not for the "natural vicissitudes of life" (here he casts the economic downturn as an act of nature and not a systemic feature of capital), Raju would not have faced the liquidity crisis that led to his failure to meet his financial obligations. In other words, had Raju's "creative" accounting practices paid off he would have been celebrated as a success! In his own words, Raju explained the experience as, "riding a tiger, not knowing how to get off without being eaten" (Economic Times Bureau 2009).

Both Raju and Das reveal to us what capitalism must feel like to the individual capitalist – a force outside his or herself, or an unpredictable tiger you cannot get off once mounted. After all, the difference between a speculator and a successful entrepreneur is decided in the market, an outcome over which the individual capitalist has no control. The resulting stress is embodied in the common sight in India where petty traders literally worship the money chest before starting work each day. For them, the market is quite literally an unpredictable god who must not be displeased. The mantra Das offers to the bourgeois caught up in the instability, ephemerality and transitory nature of global capital is this line from the *Mahabharta*: "I act because I must" (290).[10] It fits right in with the ethos of capital where what is right or wrong changes according to context. On the one hand, this relativism can support risk taking and speculation while, on the other, it can also help cope with failure, reassuring the speculator that the outcome is never in his hands.

The *Mahabharata* as a lesson for living, amidst the antagonist relations of the market, is similarly evoked in *Kahaani: A Mother of Story* (S. Ghosh 2012).[11] The movie is a thriller that casts the woman protagonist as a *karmayogi*. The moment of surprise in the film comes at the end when its protagonist, a very pregnant woman in search of her missing husband, morphs into a skilled assassin who avenges her husband's death at the hands of terrorists. All this occurs in a world whose surfaces are blindingly deceptive, dangerous and densely populated and where the lines between good and evil are deeply blurred. Furthermore, the narrative underscores a profound ethical relativism that takes deception as *de rigueur*.

Like the imagined readers of management self-help books discussed earlier, *Kahaani*'s protagonist, Vidya Bagchi (played by Vidya Balan), is also an upwardly mobile, cosmopolitan, upper-middle-class Indian. She has apparently returned from London, sporting the casual maternity clothes worn by women in the West, and is a whiz with computers. The costuming is brilliant – her flowery, little-girl maternity dresses doubly enhance her vulnerability marking her both as an outsider and a childlike woman. In contrast to the girl-like styles of Western maternity outfits, Indian women still wear the sari right through maternity. In other words, the sari does not produce the abrupt shift into girlhood achieved by Western maternity wear.

The film is set in Kolkata, and the film's cinematography and editing manage to transform the ordinary and everyday people and locations of this city into a war zone comprised of multiple antagonists and battle sites. Every character and location in this fast-paced film simmers with the expectation that it may at any time, in the blink of an eye, turn hostile. From the opening

Figure 7. Vidya Bagchi arrives in Kolkata from London. © Boundscript, Pen Movies 2012.

scene, the camera mimics the gaze of the security police or terrorist as they survey the city. For, in the end, both gazes are obsessed with the present and search for sites of disruption. Thus, they are mirror images of each other. The camera surveys the scene rapidly, darting across specific sites, dwelling only momentarily on individuals or groups, catching snatches of conversations or gestures. And thus, by breaking up the city into a montage of fragmented spaces where death may strike at any time without warning, the film manages to transform Kolkata into a war zone.

For instance, the opening scene takes place in a metro station and sets the tone of discontinuity and confusion that will mark the film. The fast-paced montage takes in the morning rush – whizzing past signs, the station clock, specific locations on the platform – and slows down momentarily to take in the security announcement over the public address system warning passengers to be wary of suspicious activity at the station. The camera dwells briefly on two interactions: the first is a group of school children who are busy teasing a child who is holding on tightly to his bag; the second is two women, with the younger one trying to pacify her crying baby while cursing herself for forgetting the milk bottle at home. A male character, not yet introduced to us, gets a phone call and we hear him ask about a bag.

Before we can hear anything further, the call is drowned in the noise as the train enters a tunnel. As the train comes out of the tunnel, the man who had just received the call slowly moves towards the group of children, his eyes on the bag the child is clutching. Meanwhile, the train comes to a stop and the woman with the baby gets off at the station leaving her bag behind. The older woman calls after her and as she holds up the bag she notices the milk bottle inside. In the flash of the second that it takes the viewer to grasp what is to transpire, a rapid succession of event unfolds. The train door closes. The bottle is thrown to the ground and erupts into a poisonous gas. The next shot is of the inside of the train, this time quiet and littered with dead bodies. The sequence closes with a long shot of the back of the train, now hurtling along into another dark tunnel. The audience, like the characters in the film, are left with the hopelessness borne of not having acted swiftly and in time.

Deception and multiple identities is a recurrent motif in the film, teaching the viewer to adopt the stance of suspicion towards all. We first see the protagonist Vidya Bagchi, arrive in Kolkata's airport from London on, what we are led to believe, is her first visit to the city. She then goes straight to the police station to file a Missing Person Report on behalf of her husband. Several twists and turns later, we learn that both the missing husband and her very visible pregnancy were a decoy to bust a terrorist conspiracy within the Indian Intelligence Bureau. Her real husband is not missing but has been dead for two years. He was, we learn, the man who received the call about a bag on the train but failed to intercept the bomb. Vidya's disguise foils the head of the Indian Intelligence Bureau, who is himself part of the terrorist network, into assigning a junior intelligence officer by the name of Khan to keep an eye on her. Khan decides on his own to use Vidya to uncover the terrorist network within the intelligence agency. He installs a police officer, Satyoki, as both her guard and the means to carry on the investigation. Eventually, it turns out that it is Vidya, under the guidance of her mentor – a retired intelligence officer – who uses the police (and not vice versa) to bust the terrorist ring inside the Intelligence Bureau. At the end, in true vigilante fashion, she imposes her own sentence – tearing away the prosthetic mask of pregnancy, she shoots the terrorist as he tries to run away.

The film casts this act of vigilantism in line with the *Mahabharata*. In a direct reference to the *Mahabharata*, the police officer assigned to assist her is named Satyoki, an ally of Arjuna and Krishna who also served as their charioteer. The film explicitly draws our attention to this allegory. On learning his name, as Satyoki drives her home from the police station on her first arrival in Kolkata, Vidya remarks: Satyoki was Arjuna's charioteer and you, as my charioteer, have been sent to help me. This way, she casts herself as Arjuna and the battle she is engaged in is as morally ambiguous as Arjuna's war with his brothers. Identities and boundaries remain in a state of flux as we learn that today's terrorist was yesterday's intelligence officer, the terrorist ring is

Figure 8. Against the Durga Puja festival, Vidya, taking the form of the goddess, shoots the alleged terrorist. © Boundscript, Pen Movies 2012. All rights reserved.

run from inside the state intelligence agency and the apparently pregnant woman is a bearer of death. This allegorical reference to the epic grants *Kahaani*'s narrative a profound moral significance, grounding its world view in an ethic sanctioned by religion and, therefore, held as transcendent, or, true for all times.

The most radical validation of ethical relativism comes at the film's climax. In the moment she assassinates the terrorist, Vidya strips off her pregnancy mask – the marker of her worldly womanly existence – and takes on the iconic form of the goddess Durga, the divine restorer of order. Wearing a red and white sari, her forehead aflame with vermillion, she shoots the terrorist, and disappears in a crowd of similarly dressed women. The voice-over narrates that when the demons, who were themselves the creation of the gods, appeared to overtake the gods, the gods created Durga to restore order. What is essentially an act of vigilantism is thus validated as a temporary restoration of order in an uncertain universe.

The protagonist draws our attention, early in the film, to the deception of surfaces and, simultaneously, the absence of anything other than images underneath the one on the surface. The veil of *Maya*,[12] when stripped, reveals only further illusion. When Vidya is first introduced to Satyoki she admiringly notes the Bengali practice of two names for the same person. Satyoki explains to her that while his official name is Satyoki, as written on his name tag, he is commonly called by his nickname, Rana. The dreaded terrorist Vidya is in search of, one by the name of Milan Dami, was himself a former intelligence officer who turned terrorist. Vidya claims he is her missing husband by photo-shopping his photo onto her wedding photograph. In a critical scene in *Kahaani*, when the investigation has led to the deaths of two innocent people

Figure 9. The iconic image of the power goddess, Durga. © Boundscript, Pen Movies 2012. All rights reserved.

and Khan is ready to put Vidya's life in danger, dismissing it as collateral damage Satyoki asks Khan,

> "What is the difference between the terrorists and us?"
>
> "Nothing," replies Khan, "It is just that we are on the right side of the law, which is what makes us right."

At the end of the film, when Vidya has finally managed to trap the terrorist in a one-on-one confrontation, he asks her,

> "What is your name?"
> "What difference does it make?" she replies.

In the morally ambiguous universe painted by the film, the individual is only a blip caught in a war without an end. Vidya's identity, like his, is without significance – and neither of the two sides can claim moral certainty. What is more, this personal insignificance and moral ambiguity is accepted pragmatically without any trace of irony, cynicism or indignation.

Time-Consciousness and the Neoliberal Subject

Moral ambiguity is premised upon a sense of personal inconsequentiality and the film makes this sense of insignificance palpably real through its depiction of the relentless speed of time. Time is sped up in the film through a series of deadlines. At each deadline, death awaits. For instance, the various characters in *Kahaani* – including the organizing gaze of the camera – must size up situations in split seconds. Moments of privacy are so rare and so patterned in the film that they further heighten the fragility of the individual against the danger lurking in the city. There are three brief sequences of Satyoki travelling alone in a tram at the end of the day; each time, he is on the phone and speaks just one brief sentence, "I'll be home, Ma." Similarly, we see only three sequences of Vidya alone in her room. There is no time for interiority as characters must always remain on guard and ready to act or risk death, both for themselves and bystanders. Human agency simply dissolves in a race against time.

There is a profound affinity between nihilism and the morally ambiguous universe painted by these contemporary readings of the *Mahabharata*. At the core of nihilism is a time-consciousness, Stanley Rosen (1969) explains, according to which the self disappears in an unyielding movement of time that incessantly destroys the present. Put differently, the present rapidly dissolves into the past and the future promises to be more of the same. Rosen further explains that this fusion of the self with a rapidly disappearing present comes from a deep-seated historicism in which all values and universals – including the desire for life – are seen as contextual.

There is something deeply nihilistic about the notion of *Maya* that undergirds contemporary interpretations of the *Mahabharata*. Understood at a popular level, the notion of *Maya* posits that this worldly and/or material life is a veil that hides another transcendental, truer metaphysical reality in which the self merges with the universe and is freed from the cycle of birth and death, otherwise known as mortality. In other words, the material world is a falsification, a dream, an illusion. Knowledge in this view, then, is not knowledge of how the world works, but rather freeing oneself of the false belief that the world is to be known, for the true nature of the world is its illusion. Ironically, while nihilism is born of a profound atheism the notion of *Maya* offers hope in the freedom of the after-life. Both regard this world, however, as incapable of redemption.

The ethical relativism, invoked in contemporary readings of the *Mahabharata* – that judgments of right and wrong are contextual and depend upon your perspective – reinforces the nihilistic perception that knowledge is ultimately limited and deceptive.[13] It further proposes that underlying all the fast and fury of the material world and the limits of one's own life, lies an unchanging, permanent "truth" or state of "bliss." The idea that everything changes and nothing changes is deeply comforting to the capitalist caught in the throes of a changing economy as well as serves as an answer to real suffering. It seems to be the theme of *Pavitra Rishta* (the Pure Relationship) (Joshi and Latkar 2010), the numerous family dramas on Indian television and of films like *Kahani*. The belief simultaneously supports renunciation – a withdrawal from the world – as well as ruthlessly taking one's chances and gambling as a way to be. At the heart of the *Mahabharata*, after all, is a game of chess and a wager in which everything is put on the line.

Ishay Landa (2007) remarked that free market liberalism is incompatible with individual freedom for its drive to economic expansion cannot grant the "sanctity of individual life" (32). Without money all become equal non-entities, part of the surplus population. Money is a cruel god – to acquire it requires an amoral, intensely competitive individual haunted by the fear of falling to the level of the masses. The Nietzchean hero, Landa elaborates, "is a crusader against the perceived leveling of mass society" (1). The vigilantism one sees on display in films like *Kahani* presents the ordinary, middle-class individual as capable to rising to this level of superiority, armed with new technologies as well as ethical relativism.

At the end of *Kahaani*, one man is dead, but the film presents both the assassinated and the assassin as interchangeable figures who would appear again, albeit in different forms and under different names. The performers are deliberately cast as ordinary, everyday people so as to de-emphasize the individual and highlight the timelessness of the narrative. Although the protagonist was played by a well-known actor, Vidya Balan, her personality does not dominate her character in the film. The individual, the film appears to say, is submerged under an onslaught of time in which the speed and impermanence of the moment is matched only by the unchanging rush of time. When asked by Satyoki if she understands the risks she is taking, if she cares for her life, Vidya replies that after her husband's death life appears to be a mere joke.

The questions that have haunted the modern psyche are: What is the meaning of my life? How can I live an authentic life? Or, in other words, live a life true to myself? As Hans Jonas (1966) explains, our sense of integrity or selfhood comes from the certain knowledge that we are mortal. In other words, it is the awareness of our finitude, which turns living for each of us into an act of freedom, where each of us must take "our lonely stand in time between the twofold nothing of before and after." It is upon this knowledge of our mortality that rests the poignancy of modern life (267).

Certain strands in postcolonial theory dismiss such thinking as Western and insist on the "difference" of a uniquely Indian time-consciousness not haunted by such pangs of the modern consciousness of one's mortality. I will discuss this position in Chapter 3. Suffice here to say that the search for meaning in the midst of a fleeting sense of time indicates, that at least the upwardly mobile cosmopolitan bourgeoisie, who have been the subject of this chapter, are no strangers to this angst of modern life. What could be more comforting to the pain of mortality than the belief that this life is itself temporary, a veil over a more permanent unity? Stated differently, the notion of *Maya* may well be seen as an old version of the advice so popular now: If you cannot change the world, then change how you think about it.

Das explains that he turned to the *Mahabharata* when he experienced his own personal time running out. He notes that middle age and aging parents all forced him to confront the question: What does this amount to? "The only certainty in the *Mahabharata*," claims Das (2009, xliii), is that "*kala* (time or death) is 'always cooking us'." In another telling anecdote, he reports asking his father, "Is there any point to life beyond the fact that we should make it to the station in time?" (296). While Das does not introspect and analyze his remark in relation to life on the corporate ladder, the remark sums the existential angst of being reduced to simply keeping time, reaching all the signposts in time, rather than, as Stanley Rosen (1999, 32–3) describes it, "occupying" it or living authentically.

To live authentically, Rosen suggests, is to make decisions in the present moment consciously, based on reason and wisdom regarding life itself. Furthermore, such liberating praxis can occur only if one has a conception of the future as open. Otherwise, one just shows up on time takes the assigned train and gets off or dies when the fated station arrives.[14] Yet, even though the latter view takes the passive conformist line, it is still premised on the belief that the way one approaches life is a matter of choice.

In the *Mahabharata*, however, both the human and the world as we know it are an illusion (or *Maya*) caught in the grip of time. What is real or permanent is time as an absolute entity and all the human can do is act according to the caste-bound rules of his or her station in life – the law of *Dharma*. In other words, time, *kala* or death are absolute while the mortal, material world is a dream or myth. The conception of the self as an individual is, in this view, false.

What might be the appeal of such time-consciousness – its insistence on human insignificance – for the bourgeois subject of neoliberalism? I suspect that the increasingly volatile market conditions of the end of the twenty-first century must drive home for the upper echelons of the bourgeoisie – the CEOs, the bankers, the marketers, etc. – a profound sense of vulnerability to conditions beyond their control. Life in capitalism, Marx said ([1845–46] 1978, 199), appeared more accidental because it was subjected to the violence of things. The evaporation of jobs, retirement savings and homes along the ups and downs of the market would certainly contribute to a sense of meaninglessness and discontinuity. Even more profoundly alienating must be the experience of self-commodification – marketing, positioning, and constantly reinventing oneself. How can the sense of individuation or uniqueness survive such incessant refashioning? The commodity can be turned over, recycled, and brought back again. But the human has only one chance at life.

The self – reduced to the insignificance of commodity – is drawn to sublimation in authoritarian projects and there is a certain zeal with which the middle class has taken upon itself to police society, especially in maintaining patriarchal order *vis-à-vis* sexuality. This fascination with authoritarian enforcement of the law finds expression in films like *Kahaani* or *A Wednesday* (Pandey 2013), which celebrate side-stepping the law and weeding out perceived threats to order. So the state does not disappear in neoliberalism, rather, not only does it deploy its muscle against its own citizens, but it produces a moral ambiguity which valorizes vigilante projects that restore order.

The commodified individual, or what Deborah Tudor (2011) has described as the "entrepreneur of the self," also fits neatly with the collapse of the model of citizenship born out of a sense of belonging to the collective. In its place is an individual who, Wendy Brown (2003) basing herself on Foucault writes, has raised market rationality to the level of a *moral value*. They cohabit in a society, that:

> figures individuals as rational, calculating creatures whose moral autonomy is measured by their capacity for "self-care" – the ability to provide for their own needs and service their own ambitions.

The ideal neoliberal subject, Brown explains, is "a 'free' subject who rationally deliberates about alternative courses of action, makes choices, and bears full responsibility for the consequences of these choices." Neoliberalism imposes, to quote Brown again, a "code of conduct" in which subjects internalize their subjectivities as entrepreneur-citizens. She explains this in terms of Foucault's notion of market rationality as governmentality, that is, "a mode of governance that encompasses but is not limited to the state, and which produces subjects, forms of citizenship and behavior, and a new organization of the social."

The model neoliberal citizen, Brown (2003) elaborates:

> [I]s one who strategizes for her/himself among various social, political and economic options, not one who strives with others to alter or organize these options. A fully realized neo-liberal citizenry would be the opposite of public-minded, indeed it would barely exist as a public. The body politic ceases to be a body but is, rather, a group of individual entrepreneurs and consumers.

It is in this context that the interpretation of the *Mahabharata* as a text that reinforces the accidental nature of life steps in to create a sense of cohesion based in Hindu cultural identity without questioning structural inequalities. In fact, it absolves bourgeois guilt, now seen as a hangover from a far distant "oppressive socialist" past.

Profits without Guilt

Once the amorality of capitalism – that is, the exploitation of each by everyone – is accepted, the grounds of the welfare state, including its paternalism, disappear. This has given a new vigor to bourgeois exploitation. I found numerous examples of this in everyday life. For instance, a young upper-middle-class woman finishes telling the day's menu to the woman who cooks for their family and turns around to explain to me:

> If we don't tell her what to make she will quickly make *dal* [a lentil] and *aalu-gobi* [potatoes and cauliflower, a common vegetable] and run off. We don't want her to *exploit* us.

What is new here is the use of the term exploitation to describe the relationship. This young woman was not charging her domestic worker with being lazy or incompetent, but rather for being a wily competitor who must be stopped from using her. Never mind the gulfs in income and opportunity or the personal history between them. The cook had been working for the family for at least a decade and a half – in fact, during the childhood of the young woman now placing the order. She still commutes an hour and a half each way to work in a number of households, such as this one, and make a lower-middle-class living for herself. The woman now placing the order has literally grown up in front of her eyes, making the shift from an uncertain, self-conscious child and college-going youngster to a young mother and career woman. Yet, that history between them has been erased by a new "professionalism" as "ma'am" places an order to the "cook" or her "chef" as she will boast in company later. It is a subtle change in language but it represents a newer, more heightened degree of separation from those who labor in the domestic sphere. The use of the title "chef" does not indicate greater professionalism for domestic work, but the aspirations of the middle class to break out of its surroundings and launch itself into the rarified atmosphere of five-star hotels.

The new emphasis on entrepreneurialism has freed the Indian bourgeoisie of its guilt. Its most visible example is micro-credit and other micro-commodities being sold to the poor. Both work on the principle that selling to the poor who are many and – as the neoliberals seem to believe – will continue to increase in numbers, can be a profitable venture. A pioneer in this regard, Hernando de Soto (1989) proclaimed that the poor were, in fact, holders of the world's wealth and should be integrated into global capital as consumers of debt and commodities. Presented as a win-win idea, micro-credit denounces social welfare as charity and imagines that everyone is a free agent in the market.

Similarly, in his theory about the fortune to be made from the bottom of the pyramid (BOP, later renamed "base of the pyramid" for political correctness), C. K. Prahalad (2006) proposed that there was a huge market waiting to be tapped, even amongst those who lived on less than $2 a day. The BOP, according to Prahalad, should be treated as consumers and the private sector should develop products (mini versions of what they sold to their upper-end market), services and distribution strategies that would enable the BOP to be a market. According to Prahalad, this would not only get rid of the reliance of the poor on government subsidies but is also a way to show respect to the poor! In other words, the working class (whether employed or structurally unemployed as a means of depressing wages overall) is asked to buy every element of its own reproduction. As an entrepreneur, everyone is supposed to make the most for themselves in an antagonist market.

Accumulation by Dispossession and the Amoral Individual

In doing so, the neoliberal state is revealing a fundamental logic of capital accumulation, which Chandra and Basu (2007), akin to David Harvey (2005), suggest is based in dispossession, that is, severing the producer from ownership of her or his means of production and turning them into an instrument of capital such that the proletariat is left with nothing to sell other than her or his labor power. This severance was, as Marx explained, the very foundation of the class and happens *not only* in the first phase of capital (as in the mid-eighteenth to nineteenth centuries when farm enclosures in England created a mass migration to the cities) but as an ongoing process constitutive of capital and on a global scale. It is "peacefully" enforced in the market through the ongoing processes of de-skilling and obsolescence that turns yesterday's bourgeois professional into today's proletariat, or through the recurrent crises of overproduction that bankrupt some capitalists and impoverish workers. However, when capital confronts a crisis or a different mode of production, it resorts to force, that is, to primitive accumulation, as in forcibly taking over land, privatizing commonly held resources and outright destruction through war.

In order to delineate what is *new* about neoliberalism, David Harvey (2005, 159) has termed the process "accumulation by dispossession" to describe the private take-over of public assets built by welfare and/or mixed economies, such as India. The new, here, should not be understood as an alternative but rather as a continuation or radicalization of the logic of capital. Neoliberalism, Harvey indicates, has so far not created new wealth and income so much as redistributed it upwards through dispossession.

The instances of dispossession in India include the Special Economic Zones (SEZs) where corporations are unfettered by the nation's labor laws. Land for these SEZs is acquired from the most marginalized groups. Tribal groups – in states such as Andhra, Chattisgarh, Jharkhand, Orissa, Bihar – who do not have private ownership in land but have inhabited it for centuries, are being forcibly displaced from lands rich in minerals. The story with which I began this chapter is located in Jharkhand which even today remains the site of violent and brutal conflict over land between those who live by it, that is, the indigenous people, and those who would rather extract its minerals and leave it deforested and impoverished, that is, the corporations such as Vedanta, Posco or Tatas. In mega-cities like Delhi and Bombay, slums are demolished and people forcibly removed from places they have built for the value of the real estate, spectacles such as the Commonwealth Games and aspirations of building "world-class" cities for global capital to converge upon.

A steady erosion of public systems in favor of business is another form of dispossession. Explaining the reasons for farmer suicides and reduced consumption of food-grains among the rural poor, Utsa Patnaik recounted in an interview (Rajalakshmi, 2008) that in the last fifteen years (1991–2006) the Indian state abandoned its policy of ensuring food security. It cut down subsidies for food grains, froze prices paid to farmers for grains, and emptied out the state's food grain reserves. Instead, farmers were encouraged to grow crops for export, such as horticulture, sugarcane, cotton, pepper and coffee. When global prices of these exports fluctuated, as they were bound to, due to competition from other Third World countries like Malaysia who offered even lower prices, many Indian farmers were left insolvent and without even food grains. Consequently, per capita food grain consumption has declined, Patnaik points out, to levels prior to World War II, or when India was under colonialism.

India Inc. and the Hollowing Out of Citizenship

While neoliberalism has thrown entire new groups into the market as surplus population, available to do any form of labor to survive and thus depress wages in general, its solution to this human crisis has been more – not less – capitalism. The neoliberal state continues to pull back on social welfare, compelling the working class to buy in ever-declining micro-bits, whatever it can afford to purchase towards sustaining its own reproduction. It is thus a class war that is on the way to turning every form of reproduction into a micro-commodity you have to buy – water, medicine, food, roads, education, etc., etc. It garners legitimacy, within a broader market rationality, that has turned governance into an exercise in marketing the nation. Updating Adam Smith's *Comparative Advantage of Nations* to the present, Michael Porter (1990) advanced the catchy title – *Competitive Advantage of Nations* – advising nations to position themselves as brands, to specialize in and develop certain areas. "A nation's standard of living," Porter explains, "depends upon the capacity of its companies to achieve high levels of productivity – and to increase productivity over time" (76). For examples, Porter cites the following: German autos and chemicals, Swiss banking and pharmaceuticals, Italian footwear and textiles and US commercial aircrafts and motion pictures, and ends by charmingly patting South Korea for its pianos.

Brand India advertises a mix of the new (information technology, medical tourism) and the old (Indian art, fashions and tourism, leather, gems, *Ayurveda*). To stay ahead in the race, nations should, Porter advises, take a global approach which may even require that they, "[…] locate production or R&D facilities in other nations to take advantage of lower wage rates, to gain or improve market access, or to take advantage of foreign technology" (78). Each Indian state now competes for its brand identity to put out, as Jairam Ramesh states, "a cafeteria of smaller or sub brands" (in Narayan Ramesh 2005). There is, for instance, Gujarat for medical tourism, Kerela for *Ayurveda*, Tiruppur for hosiery and Ludhiana for woolens. There is, he says, in fact no Brand India. "There is Brand Bangalore, there's a Brand Hyderabad, there's a Brand Chennai, there's a Brand Kolkata – whatever that stands for. But it is a brand." In the same vein, Shashi Tharoor (2007), India's representative to the United Nations, extols the rise of India as the world's supermarket, selling here and there:

> The exports of Bollywood are reaching beyond NRIs [Non-resident Indians] to foreign audiences. And Indian food has gone global. In England today, Indian curry houses employ more people than coal, iron, and steel and shipbuilding industries combined. So, the Empire can strike back.

Hannah Arendt (1968), reading Marx, pointed out that capital accumulation cannot take place in the absence of a political structure – capitalists need the state to formulate laws and financial systems, to back them with police power, surveillance and a monopoly of the instruments of violence. Fully acknowledging this relationship between capital and the state, Porter (1990) confirms in no uncertain language that, "nations have become more, not less, important in a world of increasingly global competition" (73). Companies are based in nation states and nations "provide an environment that enables companies to improve and innovate faster than foreign rivals" (77).

The theory of India as a great global power represents the global aspirations of its bourgeoisie – the wish that it would escape from Indians to join a transnational bourgeoisie. This has proven to be true for some – such as the two who made it on *Fortune* magazine's list of 50 Most Powerful Women in Business in 2003 (TNN 2003),[15] the 47 who made it on *Forbes*' list of the world's billionaires (Kroll and Dolan 2013), the CEOs of multinationals and the entrepreneurs who have residences in various parts of the globe. Terms such as "Planet India" or claims such as Gurcharan Das' "India Unbound" (2001) fly off the shoulders of this class.

For the most part though, the claim to global greatness appears to be, as Achin Vinayak (2004) notes, on the wane. The will to escape history as a class and achieve the kind of wealth accumulated by the Global North is now, as Randhir Singh (1999) has realistically assessed, simply out of reach. The Indian bourgeoisie, Singh concludes, has neither the advantages of an imperialist past nor the profits amassed following World War II, which saw the ascendancy of the US. In comparison to China – which Samir Amin (2005) suggests developed, under its "really existing socialism," a far more thorough-going improvement in social infrastructure, popular standard of living and higher growth rates – the state-centered development model practiced in India remained overwhelmingly limited to its middle class. As the paternalistic state has increasingly minimized or outsourced its welfare role, the middle class has shrunk, splitting between those who have made it and those who could not and the notion of citizenship is giving way to regional, religious or caste-based identities.

We can see this political-economic shift in popular cultural texts, which are in the midst of reimagining the ending to Devi's story. In the newly popular thriller genre, India's arrested development serves as a backdrop – a shockingly vivid, uncertain and transient mise-en-scène – against which protagonists make their mark in a brief and temporary life. No tears of self-loathing or awakening into history from one's previous delusions about the nation haunt them. All that counts is risk, speed, action and, ultimately, a nihilistic faith in the meaninglessness of life. As the tagline of a recent commercial Hindi film, *Rush* (S. Desai 2012) goes: He who does not take a risk will find that everything will turn risky for him; If you stop... you die.

Chapter 3

FOR SOME DREAMS A LIFETIME IS NOT ENOUGH: THE *RASA* AESTHETIC AND THE EVERYDAY IN NEOLIBERALISM

A recent Hindi film dialogue that has caught the popular imagination goes something like this: "If it is not happy, then it cannot be the end. The film has yet to be continued, my friend." The refrain runs through *Om Shanti Om* (Khan et al. 2007), a film whose tagline, "For some dreams a lifetime is not enough," indicates that the end may be postponed even beyond a lifetime. *Om Shanti Om*'s circuitous plot celebrates a love-affair with cinema over two generations and lifetimes. The film's protagonist Om, played by the current reigning star Shah Rukh Khan, is cast as a lowly film-extra in the 1970s who hopes, one day, to be a big star and win the love of the leading female star of the period. He eventually fulfills both those dreams – but in another lifetime. Reborn as the son of a major star, Khan is reincarnated as the leading star of the new century. The narrative, thus, puts its finger on one of the most distinctive pleasures of Hindi cinema, that is, the promise of a happy ending while simultaneously postponing it. It would not be far-fetched to say that, if only it were possible to do so, Hindi cinema would indefinitely postpone the appearance of "The End."

"The film has yet to reach its end," has now passed on into everyday expression. When used as a metaphor for life itself, it suggests that life is a tale of twists and turns that will in the end – defined in the vaguest possible way – resolve themselves. Shah Rukh Khan recited that dialogue on his television quiz show as consolation to a contestant who was leaving the game after having lost it. Reminding her of her impending wedding and wishing her well, he advised her: "The film has yet to end, my friend." To be clear, Khan was not suggesting that the wedding would be the end of the contestant's life. The wedding may well be the happy culmination of a relationship or the arrangements that went into the marriage, but the implication of Khan's statement was that it too would be only a temporary stop in her life. What is significant here is that while the end is deferred indefinitely, it is not replaced with a state of limbo. Instead, what is on offer are a series of intermittent and temporary endings that help defer or, one might say, indefinitely postpone the final ending.

While I will argue that the fascination with the deferral of closure resonates with India's shift to neoliberalism, the convention is itself not new. Rather, what we are seeing is a reinvigorated enthusiasm for an aesthetic that favors stretching time and an indifference to deadlines and closures. It may be observed, for instance, in the typically longer length of Hindi movies. Stretching a film is itself seen as a draw and audiences speak of value realized if their time in the theater is filled with worthy attractions.[1] The fun lies in the twists, coincidences and cues that serve to reassure the spectator of an overall, vague movement towards resolution while drawing out the time in-between. The standard feature of the interval is another case in point. As Lalitha Gopalan (2002) explained, the interval appears as a temporary halt in the narrative, where one story ends and another begins. Gopalan, in fact, described popular Hindi cinema as the "aesthetic of interruptions."

Similarly, Madhava Prasad (1998) notes the general absence of an overriding vision or narrative arch in popular Hindi cinema and attributes it to production practices which he characterizes as the "heterogeneous mode of production." Prasad elaborates that each of the elements of popular Hindi film form – for example: music, song, dialogue and stars – carries its own weight, such that the resulting film is more an assembly of autonomously produced parts rather than the result of an overarching authorial vision. For instance, music composers, dialogue writers and stars are important figures in their own right and we have the situation where scenes are being written on set.

The textual politics of such cinema, Prasad argues, subordinates individuation – that is, the psychological development of protagonists – and helps reproduce a pre-modern feudal public where privilege is preferred over merit and kinship and blood loyalties over free association. Along these lines, Prasad explains that couples do not kiss in Hindi cinema because it would grant primacy to the sexual or conjugal relationship, thus undermining the authority of the extended familial or social relationships over the individual. In other words, the conventions of Hindi cinema replay what Prasad calls "the feudal family romance," that is, they refuse privacy and other forms of individualistic psychic identification that would threaten feudal scopic regimes.

This is not to say that there is no erotic display in Hindi cinema – the songs and dances are ample evidence of it. Yet, these sequences are as much about expressing and exploring individual desire as they are about interpolating individual desire within the discourses of the nation, family or ruminations over human life itself. The typical Holi number, a common feature in popular Hindi films, is a case in point.[2] It is undoubtedly presented as a spectacle of color and sexual energy, including varying degrees of machismo. It also takes the narrative forward. At the same time, it also encourages a reflection on or expression of collective desires associated with spring – new beginnings, beauty, friendship, hope and, of course, romantic and sexual love. Hindi film songs can so easily slip into everyday life not only because they are derived from popular and folk music, but also because they perform the social in the movies themselves.

As Ravi Vasudevan (2000) explains, the conventions of frontality, iconicity and tableau emphasize the film as a spectacle placed in front of the audience. Illusory realism, so central to the classical Hollywood narrative, is eschewed here in favor of an aesthetic that showcases cinema as a performance and does not seek individualistic immersion into the story-world on the screen. The audience of the popular Hindi film, Vasudevan explains, is addressed as a public through direct address. In contrast, the classical Hollywood narrative, as Christian Metz (1977) indicated all those years ago, addresses the individual inviting psychological identification with film and positions the spectator as an invisible presence within the film itself. Subsequently, the required norm in classical Hollywood spectatorship is to be quiet in the theater so as not to disturb the illusion that one is watching alone.

The Hindi film addresses its audience as a collective in multiple ways. For instance, the beginning of the film serves as an invocation or call to viewing – the censor board certificate signifying the film has been cleared for viewing, the roll of credits including thank you notes and often-times a narration or a verse that opens and then ends the film. Another element of direct address is the practice of inserting numerous references to the epics, casting the narrative as one already known to the audience.[3] Finally, the audience, also called the "public" in popular parlance, is invited to perform the act of spectatorship – to sing, dance, or speak back to the screen.

Since cinema theaters have, over the course of the twentieth century in India, been largely masculinist spaces, the self-exhibition of performance was largely appropriated by men, particularly the urban male proletariat who would interact with the screen with song, dance and loud commentary. This is changing in multiplexes where the urban male proletariat is blocked out first through price and then the overt presence of policing by security guards and surveillance cameras. In the resulting enclosure, the middle class has claimed – to a certain extent even across gender – the fun of the commercial Bombay film, responding physically with whistles and claps, for example, to the action on the screen.[4]

When the same aesthetic of direct address is brought into the home via the television screen, it enables the performance of spectatorship in relation to the power dynamics within the family. For instance, watching melodramatic soaps on television with the family are a subtle but clear way to articulate tensions within the family. Ranging from bodily cues to direct commentary, daughters-in-law can, for example, express pleasure in the humiliations of on-screen mothers-in-laws in front of their own extended family. It is now on television and, in particular, in melodramatic serials (rather than in cinema) that the conventional aesthetics of Bombay cinema, including the heterogeneous mode of production, subordination of individuation and deferral of closure are now abundantly on display.[5] Although started in the 1980s, the soaps received a new lease on life with the deregulation of Indian television in the 1990s as a state-owned enterprise and the subsequent opening of Indian television to global media conglomerates and Bombay cinema.[6] A proliferation of channels ensued and with it an increase in the hours of television up till the present, when television occupies 24 hours a day, 7 days a week.[7] These serials, as they are called, focus primarily on the domestic lives of the middle and upper-middle class or the rural landlord bourgeoisie caught in a period of change.

The Temporal Patterns of *Pavitra Rishta*

In order to fully explore the temporal nature of the television soap and how it resonates with the time-consciousness of neoliberalism, I will take the series *Pavitra Rishta* (the Pure Relationship) (Joshi and Latkar 2010) as a case in point. The series began in June 2009 and was still on the air at the time of this writing, October 2012. It is telecast five days a week with each episode, including advertisements, lasting 30 minutes. The show follows the fortunes of Archana, the eldest of three daughters and a son, from a lower-middle-class Maharashtrian family living in a Bombay *chawl*.[8] This distinguishes the serial from others of this genre that are preoccupied with the lives and homes of the wealthy.

Nevertheless, its representation of urban lower-middle-class life is rife with ideological mystifications and, like other shows, is primarily made for the middle- to upper-middle-class audience. This may be observed from the ads that are interspersed throughout the series. Ranging from soaps, shampoos, toothpastes, energy products for children and life insurance policies, the ads emphasize the middle-class ethic of self-improvement. Taken together, these serials may be read for the anxieties and hopes of middle-class life for whom both the lives of the very wealthy and those in the *chawls* remain largely a mystery and thus open to self-projection.

The heroine of *Pavitra Rishta* is Archana and, like others in this genre, her life is a series of tests that call for the greatest sacrifices, which she submits to with unwavering resolve. When her mother falls ill, Archana drops out of school to take care of the family and embarks on a lifetime of sacrificing for others. She mirrors her mother, who too has lived for others – although the mother expresses her ambivalence about constantly sacrificing for others at certain key points in the series. For example, in the 30 June 2010 episode, one year into the show, the ambivalence about self-denial is played out once again as Archana cries out to her mother that all she ever wanted from life was to be an ordinary girl. She asks: "Why must I suffer so? Why am I like this – that I seek my happiness in the joys of others?" The mother replies that she too has lately been asking the same questions. While at one time she would have said, with the greatest pride, that her daughter was the best, she now wishes that her daughter had not been so nice. Archana's adopted daughter, Poorvi, is the third generation in this saga of sacrificing women and perhaps, the most sacrificing of all. An orphan who is adopted by Archana as a baby, Poorvi sacrifices the love of her life, Arjun, to her sister and even gives up her newborn to them.

In a rags-to-riches fantasy, Archana's husband Manav, a car mechanic, goes on to – through twists of fate and hard work – become a wealthy business man whose business traverses India and Canada. Manav and Archana are the *Jodi* (couple) that the title, *Pavitra Rishta*, refers to. Manav, like Archana, puts others ahead of himself and this results in a series of misunderstandings that keep them apart. He, too, articulates his ambivalence about following the moral codes of middle-class life that demand self-sacrifice and deferral of pleasure. For instance, in the 24 October 2010 episode, Manav articulates his frustration at having to work under humiliating conditions:

> We middle-class people have no future. We can neither live in palaces like these rich people nor on the streets like the poor. We have to think about our families at the cost of our self-respect. First we cannot find a job and, when we do, we do not even have the power to leave it.

Yet, the desire for justice and closure is stalled through a series of mirroring patterns that reinforce the cyclical and repetitious nature of time. Hardly one problem is resolved for Archana and Manav before another befalls them. This brings us to another similarity shared by devoted couples on this show – they are all compelled to stay apart. Manav and Archana live apart for eighteen years due to misunderstandings sown by his mother. Archana's mother spends many years as a widow. Archana's daughter, Poorvi, loses Arjun to her sister. Then, there is the pattern of triangles that threaten marriages. Upon learning of his younger brother's death, Manav – who is already married to Archana –

decides to divorce her so that he can marry his younger brother's pregnant girlfriend, Shravani. Vaishali, Archana's younger sister, struggles with a husband who was already married to another woman. Separations, meetings and then separations again are presented as a cyclical pattern of family life.

The recurrent motif of love and loss is echoed in another ongoing theme – the bond between mothers and daughters and rivalries between sisters that tear at those bonds. Of the three daughters, Archana is the closest to her mother. Yet, the major source of anguish in her life, besides her mother-in-law, is her sister, Varsha. Unable to have a child, Varsha kidnaps Archana's son and keeps him with her for eighteen years. Of Archana's three daughters, Ovi covets Poorvi's love and manages to blackmail her way into marrying him. The two sisters also have only one child between them. The same patterns repeat themselves over two generations; the same story is told again and again.

Ultimately, repetition is presented as the law of life itself. *Pavitra Rishta* positions the Hindu god Ganesha (Ganapati), or *bappa* (father) as he is affectionately called by the various families whose lives are entwined in the show, as the penultimate screenwriter. Ganesha's altar has pride of place in the two homes that form the core of the story, characters address *bappa* and shot-reverse-shot sequences animate Ganesha as a witness to the family drama, presenting Ganesha as an unpredictable, but ultimately benevolent, writer of human destiny. Ganesha represents time itself, manifested as cyclical and repetitive. As a figure in the fictional world of *Pavitra Rishta*, he is both inside the drama as well as above it; as a god he embodies timelessness in the everyday. Stated differently, Ganesha is inserted into the everyday and, in turn, the everyday is infused with timelessness.

Figure 10. *Pavitra Rishta*, 13 November 2010. The title on the left of the frame translates to "next week," forecasting the reunion that is to occur the following week. This is not the first or last reunion to occur on this show and Ganesha, as witness, cements meeting and parting as the law of life, itself. © 2010 Zee TV. All rights reserved.

Figure 11. One of several shot-reverse-shots with Ganesha. Here Manav addresses Ganesha in the 13 November 2010 episode. © 2010 Zee TV. All rights reserved.

Figure 12. And in the following shot, Ganesha looks back, as if listening. © 2010 Zee TV. All rights reserved.

This is not to suggest that the soap presents the individual as a mere spectator of life performing a predestined script. As the virtuous, especially women characters, repeatedly state in the series: one must live one's life fully, fleeting as it is, and leave the rest to *bappa*. For example, Archana, whose life is an eternal saga of losing her husband and the family she loves so much, speaks of gathering memories, savoring the brief moments, or *pal*, that she gets to spend with them so that she may be able to survive the long and inevitable separations. In other words, the series recommends a double perception – that of being both a spectator and a participant in the drama of one's life. In terms of time-consciousness, it teaches that time follows a cyclical pattern where moments of happiness are interspersed with sadness.

In fact, *Pavitra Rishta* has a character that mirrors Ganesha's double location – as simultaneously present both in the drama and outside it in a more diminutive and human form. This part is played by the male lead, Manav's father, Damodar Deshmukh, who has some characteristics of a *sutradhar* (narrator). According to aesthetics of Indian theater, the *sutradhar* is a figure who intercedes between the audience and the performance, acts as a witness or observer of the drama, and may well be the director or screenwriter. The *sutradhar* often introduces or performs the invocations prior to starting the performance as well as ends the performance. He, as is generally the case, may also show up at critical moments in the drama to comment or observe. In a metaphysical sense, the *sutradhar* may well be considered time itself, as the puppeteer who holds the strings of human drama. Literally translated, *sutradhar* means, "one who holds the threads."

Cast as a professional playwright and actor, Damodar Deshmukh repeatedly evokes his own writing skills as well as those of Ganesha, to comment on the twists in the series. Often, at critical moments in the drama, Damodar stands aside and observes, shows approval or disapproval for, and judges the characters. In a tongue-in-cheek reference to the many twists and travails of the female lead in the soap, Archana, he tells her,

> "Seeing the ups and downs in your lives, I feel like writing a play on your life."
> "Who? My life!" she demurs. "There is nothing extraordinary about my life."[9]

The series is also well aware of and pokes fun at the unrealistic nature of its extravagant melodramatic plots, thus drawing attention to and enacting its own performance. The mother-in-law, who is the loudest character in the show, often chides the others for taking pleasure in her fights as if she were a "character in a serial." The show also has a blatant disregard for continuity. For instance, a leap of twenty years in the show was not accompanied by grey hair on actors and actresses. Furthermore, characters are simply dropped out of the show. In the last six months of 2012, the youngest of Archana's three sisters simply disappeared from the show, while one of her sons continued to show up now and then. The actor playing Archana's youngest sister was changed and, even more strikingly, the actor playing the male lead as Manav (Sushant Singh Rajput) was changed more than two years into the show. All it

Figure 13. Manav no. 1, played by Sushant Singh Rajput. © 2010 Zee TV. All rights reserved.

Figure 14. Manav no. 2, played by Hiten Tejwani. © 2012, Zee TV. All rights reserved.

took to insert the new actor (Hiten Tejwani) in the role were a few flashbacks restaging the past and the show was continued.

Yet, changing actors does not disrupt the flow of the narrative because it is not organized around individual psychological states but around iconic characters – such as sacrificing women, devoted couples and the significance of relationships. In one episode, for example, Archana, lamenting that her daughter Poorvi had taken on sacrificing for others, cries out that she had never wanted "another Archana" to be born. These circuitous and repetitive plot lines suggest that the struggles of the individual are, in fact, not unique to particular individuals. For instance, a standardized feature of the soaps is the time jump – the story reaches an impasse and is picked up again twenty or so years later only to repeat the unresolved conflicts from before.

Since the same themes run through most melodramas, one gets the sense that, other than different casts and settings, the stories are interchangeable. In fact, the producers admit as much. There is, for instance, the regular feature called the *mahasangam* or *maha*-episode, that is, the grand union or episode in which different soaps are merged and characters intervene in each other's lives and offer advice or help resolve the immediate concern at hand. Zee TV, the site of the most popular channel for such family soaps, has the tag line: *Har pal banaye ik naya rishta* (Every moment brings a new relationship), suggesting that its soaps, like life, are all part of one large family melodrama.

Part of the reason for the merging of characters and plots is simply economic – mass production with an eye on cutting costs. Production houses like Balaji, under the supervision of Ekta Kapoor, are responsible for an overwhelming majority of such fare, including soaps with interchangeable plots and themes such as *Kyunki Saas Bhi Kabhi Bahu Thi* (Because the Mother-in-Law was also Once a Daughter-in-Law), *Kahaani Ghar Ghar Kii* (The Story of Every Family), *Kasautii Zindagii Kay* (The Stakes of Life), *Kahin to hoga* (Somewhere There Must Be), *Kkusum, Kaahin Kissii Roz* (Someday Somewhere), *Kitani Mohabbat Hai* (How Strong is Your Love), *Kya Huaa Tera Vaada* (Where Did Your Promises Go) and *Kis Desh Mein Hai Mera Dil* (In Which Country Does My Heart Reside). Produced according to the assembly line logic of economies of scale, writers cross over and so do stars. Ekta Kapoor (2007) who has produced 40 serials with 15 currently in production, explained the production process as follows:

> There hasn't been much time to ponder what's happened and what's happening with a so-called scenario. I wake up in the morning and think about what I am actually going to put in my shows and go ahead and do that. I'm battling actor problems; I'm battling on-set problems […].

Stereotypical plots and the highly codified nature of melodramatic acting, dialogue, scenarios and cinematography make it possible to churn out shows in quick succession and solidify the impression of unity across different episodes and serials. For instance, in terms of acting, there are standard gestures – such as taking the hand to the mouth to express surprise or taking both hands to the temples to express anguish. A particular feature of cinematography is the bullet zoom – a series of narrowing, punctuated zooms that depict shock. Dramatic moments are underlined with loud music, including repetitious patterns of chanting passages from Hindu religious texts as well as specific tunes associated with people. In other words, both the practices of production and the form create the impression that the soaps are all telling the same story.

Television Melodrama and Women's Domestic Labor

The movement of time in these soaps is ultimately repetitious and cyclical. The resolution of one dramatic episode, for instance, merely leads to yet another problem in the ongoing family drama. Occasionally, concurrently run soaps merge and characters from one soap appear in another soap as if the families are interconnected in one large continuous melodrama. Each series often lasts several years with plots that are in synch with the seasons and rituals outside, thus further enhancing a cyclical awareness of time. And, set as they are within the domestic sphere, the soaps enact the repetitious and cyclical rhythms of household routines. Household routines – such as morning prayers, making tea, cutting vegetables, etc. – are interspersed in these shows alongside the family drama.

Thus, the absence of a narrative arch is filled with a circular flow of time based in season and ritual. For instance, a shot of the rising sun is used as a recurrent motif in *Pavitra Rishta* to mark another day. Or, there is the repeated shot of the Dombivili train station, presenting that reliable marker of time in Bombay, that is, the local train in which the working class spends so much of its time. With the onset of winter, Poorvi and her grandmother dust out the blankets and comment on the unusually chilly winter in Bombay that year – true to the real life weather.

Festivals such as Holi, Diwali and Ganapati Puja are celebrated by the characters in step with these celebrations in viewers' homes and used sometimes to stage some major development in the story. For instance, the festival of Holi in March 2013 became an occasion to develop a critical turning point in the relationship between Archana and Manav and Arjun and Poorvi. Characters started to mention the coming of Holi a week before the event. On-screen preparations were used to build anticipation around possible reconciliation between the estranged couples as well as parents and children. Would Manav accept Poorvi as his daughter and recognize his other daughter, Teju, who, unknown to him, is also in Bombay at this time? Would Arjun and Poorvi express their attraction to each other? At the climactic moment of this particular mini-plot, Poorvi and Arjun get caught by a group of revelers and play Holi, as do Manav and Archana in their community compound. Poorvi gets her blessings from Manav and Archana as does Teju from her father. In the spectacular play of color and people, relationships are momentarily resolved and the vivid experience of life is savored.

Repetition is, of course, written into the daily household routines of eating, sleeping, cleaning, and going to work. As Nancy Chodorow (1978) has indicated, the work of maintenance and reproduction is repetitive, routine and lacking in a defined sense of progression and product. For example, you clean the dishes after one meal and they are ready to be cleaned after the next. Moreover, domestic labor involves continuous responsiveness to demands on time set by others, that is, a baby needing to be fed or attending to a knock at the door. The pleasures of daytime soaps for women, Tania Modleski (1984) writes, is the congruence between the relational, distracted and interrupted rhythms of household routines and the storylines of television soaps. Modleski elaborates that soaps are obsessed with relationships – their plot details and aesthetic elements, such as wordy dialogues and close-ups, are fixated on reading other people's minds. This is very true of *Pavitra Rishta*. The characters are always listening in on others' conversations or guessing what is going on in others' minds. Even in a large city like Bombay, they invariably manage to run into each other.

Such intense preoccupation with others' states of mind and emotional needs is very much women's work within the patriarchal domestic sphere. The connection between the ideal woman and her knowledge of the needs and thoughts of her family is made directly in *Pavitra Rishta* with an oft-repeated shot of the kitchen window as a vantage point from where the household may be observed. Most often occupied by Archana, it is also at various critical times occupied by other women. Modleski concludes that soaps are meaningful for women because their formats, including deferred resolutions, repetitive plot lines and preoccupation with others, echo women's work in the household. She writes:

> My point is that a distracted or distractable frame of mind is crucial to the housewife's efficient functioning in her real situation, and at this level television and its so-called distractions, along with the particular forms they take, are intimately bound up with women's work. (1984, 74)

While I agree with Modleski that soaps are pleasurable to women because they echo the rhythms of housework as well as the emotional work women do in the family, I find that contemporary Hindi soaps go one step further. They imbue the repetitiveness of everyday routines with an awareness of the cyclical and this, I believe, ideologically produces the domestic sphere as the "other" of the commodified sense of time that governs the market and makes the latter bearable.

The Everyday in Capitalism

Analyzing the temporal consciousness of daily life, Henri Lefebvre (1987) explains that there are two modes of repetition which intersect in the everyday. One is cyclical – as in nature with its seasons and rituals that follow the seasons, birth and death, day and night. The other is linear or rational – as in the repetitive gestures of work and consumption. While the first alludes to timelessness, that is, time before and after the individual, the latter – tied as it is to the linear logic of the clock – accentuates the finitude of individual life. As Lefebvre clarifies:

> In modern life, the repetitive gestures tend to mask and to crush the cycles. The everyday imposes its monotony. It is the invariable constant of the variations it envelops. The days follow one another and resemble one another and yet – and here lies the contradiction at the heart of everydayness – everything changes. But the change is programmed: Obsolescence is planned. Production anticipates reproduction; production produces change in such a way as to superimpose the impression of speed on that of monotony. Some people cry out against the acceleration of time, others cry out against stagnation. They're both right. (10)

Stated differently, it is the cyclical that offers relief from the repetitive routines of work and consumption that, in alienated relations of capital, appears to consume our time which, ultimately, is finite.

E. P. Thompson (1967) offers an astute analysis of the relation between capitalism and the anxiety around the passing of time. Thompson argues that industrial capitalism imposed a new form of time-discipline, producing time as an abstract, homogeneous entity that could be broken up and exchanged in the market. It replaced an earlier task-orientation in which time was not an abstraction but interconnected with place and the task at hand, that is, the amount of time spent on a task was determined by the needs of that job and not the external, mechanical and linear logic of the clock against which wages and profits were calculated. Tasks on the assembly line, or now in global networks of production, are broken up and fragmented, labor is paid in exchange for the socially determined value of labor time and the value of one's time depends upon one's position in the market. Whereas, precapitalist time-consciousness, Thompson indicates, was marked by a certain indifference and submission to the passing of time, the production of time as a commodity in capitalism produces an acute awareness of it being "wasted," "spent" or "lost." Time literally comes to be understood as a currency and the individual filled with an acute awareness of life, itself, as a ticking clock with an expiration date.

Such an acute awareness of time as currency has been radicalized in neoliberalism, as the work of self-production has become a continuous and ongoing project for the middle-class subject. From child-rearing to education, every activity is seen as an investment or entrepreneurial venture performed in hopes of some future return. And time not spent furthering such goals as a lost opportunity. While an enhanced consciousness of the everyday was itself a product of capitalism and premised upon the separation of home as a private sphere, the home is now increasingly overtaken by market time discipline. E. P. Thompson had remarked that task-orientation still continued to be observed in domestic routines – for example, childcare follows the needs of the child that cannot be fully timed to the clock.

Yet, the notion of time as currency has very much infused the fiber of everyday life through the neoliberal notion of incessant self-production and management for maximum returns. This is very much in evidence in parental "investment" in children, something that children internalize as well. The speed-up of time that ensues from seeing every second as an opportunity lost for self-advancement may be observed in the ads that punctuate *Pavitra Rishta*. For example, an ad for the soap Lifebuoy has a group of children teasing another nerdy one for taking too long to wash his hands. "Your soap must be slow," they giggle. Or there is an ad for toothpaste which boasts of needing only "two minutes" for brushing. And, there is an ad for a Honda motorcycle. Paraphrasing the jingle, it goes something like this: Speed is our dream and it is also our truth; we wake up in the morning and bow to the clock.

The appeal of shows like *Pavitra Rishta* is that they suppress the simultaneous monotony and speed of everyday life in capitalism and imbue it, instead, with a flow of time that veers towards the cyclical. As I have argued here, this is grounded in certain formal attributes of the Indian cinematic tradition which have carried over into the television soaps that emphasize the collective over the individual and timelessness over the finitude of individual life. A cyclical time-consciousness is premised upon a certain forgetfulness of the self that is grounded in a form of socialization that, Stanley Kurtz (1992) and others have noted, favors renunciation over acquisition. According to Sudhir Kakkar (1978), the governing principle of Hindu self-realization is *Moksha* or freedom from the individualist cycle of birth and rebirth towards unity with the universe and life in general. In other words, Kakkar writes, "Man's ultimate meaning is not realized until a person also has a similar feeling of 'I' in the selves of others" (19). While it is doubtful that soaps like *Pavitra Rishta* teach renunciation, their cyclical narratives do de-center the self – offering relief from the crushing questions regarding the meaning of individual life and the loss of one's lifetime in everyday routines of work and consumption.

The concept of *Rasa* enhances both a de-centering of the self as well as absorption in an experience of time as something to be savored, not used up.[10] In terms of Indian performance aesthetics, this translates into teaching a lesson in detachment from this world as well as one's subjective experience of it by considering both as mere illusion or *Maya*. Life then must be imagined as a play (*leela*) of fate. Indian art, Kakkar indicates, was traditionally dominated by the goal of creating (by the artist), evoking (in the audience) and absorption (by both) of *Rasa* (1978, 30). *Rasa* literally means taste, essence or flavor and is oriented towards producing emotional states and experiences. It is the emphasis on experiencing states of consciousness that suspends the onward rush of time, turns the interruptions themselves into the attractions, and treats the passing of time with abandon. The point of these soaps, as I have indicated, is not to develop suspense around narratives. Instead, it is to suspend the angst of losing time that is implicit in everyday routines. Yet, the pain is dulled, not by offering the present as a space of individual and collective transformation, but rather as an illusion. Thus, attempts to change the world appear futile.

Future Denial

The disavowal of the present as a space of action may be best recognized by analyzing the presentation of the future in these soaps. The future, which is always at stake in deferred gratification – after all, the entire point of waiting is to obtain better results in the future – is, in these cyclical renderings, simply just more of the same. Even Archana asks occasionally, "When will our problems end?" But the point these soaps make is that problems are, in fact, never ending; that, while the desire for justice or happiness is intense, it is ultimately unobtainable. These soaps achieve what a film, because of its nature as a text with a beginning and an end, cannot – that is, they defer the ending to a point where the ending itself becomes insignificant.

These long running soaps simply end one day with scant regard for resolution. For instance, *Teen Bahuraniya* (Three Daughters-in-Law) (Joshi et al. 2007), a soap that ran from March 2007 to January 2009 and extended over 371 episodes, abruptly ended its winding plot that included terrorist attacks, ghosts and a suicide. In its last episode, the female head of the household, along with her on-screen family including the three suddenly pregnant daughters-in-law, simply faced the camera and said goodbye "to your family from ours."

Deferred Endings and Neoliberalism

It may be argued that the time-consciousness of these soaps is an instance of alternative temporalities that cannot be accommodated within homogeneous – some would even characterize as Western or colonial – time.[11] Such an argument would overlook the global nature of capitalism. Moreover, when applied to the particular example of television soaps and their primarily middle- to upper-middle-class audience, the notion of difference simply fails to account for the fact that both the production practices of these soaps as well as their audiences are fully integrated into capitalism. The pacing of these shows, the constant switch between melodramatic change and the stability of relationships, echoes rather well with the demands on the neoliberal subject to postpone pleasure and control impulsive behavior while simultaneously participating in constant reinvention – a process in which the boundaries around the public and private, and one's interior and exterior self, are relentlessly blurred.

Capitalism demands the inner coherence, which would compel individuals to show up to work on time and pay their debts, while at the same time requires them to reinvent themselves in response to the uncertainties of the global labor market as well as the lures of consumer culture. "Do something new today," shout the billboards of shopping malls, such as Shopper's Stop in Bombay, and "I reinvented myself" is a badge of honor for the middle-aged executive whose career has spanned the two-and-a-half decades of neoliberalism. The privatization unleashed in the '80s brought with it a new-found respect for the MBA as a sought-after degree for the nation's brightest graduates.[12] The careers of those alumni have followed the twists of the market: beginning with an Indian corporate house, moving into a multinational, the middle-aged executive now describes him/herself as a self-employed entrepreneur who dreams of one day becoming a "gamechanger."[13]

In other words, "Reinvent yourself while staying the same!" is the contradictory demand placed upon middle-class time-consciousness by its conditions of labor and consumption. As labor, the middle class produces surplus value by postponing pleasure while, as purchasers of commodity culture, it must pursue immediate gratification. The constant struggle is to acquire new skills and stay ahead of the de-professionalization and subsequent proletarianization unleashed by the contemporary phase of capital, which has global labor at its disposal and new technologies which have made it immensely mobile and capable of extracting surplus value from across the globe. Such is the constant disruption of middle-class life. There are temporary pauses, celebrations, victories and defeats, but the "fear of falling" into the ranks of the proletariat, which Barbara Ehrenreich (1990) identified as the existential angst of middle-class life, is never-ending. The picture has yet to reach its end, my friend, and therefore the best way to deal with it is to keep working till you get the desired end!

Even the most wanted subject of the advertiser and marketer – that is, the purchaser of goods and services – must practice deferral (although the ads seem to suggest otherwise). The fully realized purchaser of commodity culture, or one not given to self-denial or sacrifice, would not show up to work or pay bills in time and so jam the capitalist ethos of ceaseless work. Ultimately, however, such a subject would also be a wrench in the cycle of commodity culture. For the endless purchasing required of capitalist consumer culture also relies on and builds in a lingering state of dissatisfaction. Each purchase, in other words, must leave the individual wanting more. Ultimately, capitalism builds in and thrives on an incessant deferral of pleasure.

Inner Engineering and the Self and World as *Maya*

The indefinite postponement of pleasure – the incessant pressure to reinvent oneself in response to the demands of a changing reality – must reach a point where reality itself begins to seem like an illusion or *Maya*. Television soaps are one kind of object lesson in practicing a life of such decentering. The other is offered by the increasing number of religious based self-help gurus who have emerged in India. One such program, tellingly named "Inner Engineering," run by Sadhguru analyzes depression as the result of the false belief that the world can be changed according to one's desires. In its place, the program offers to teach "technologies of well being" that can bring about an inner transformation to help deal with a "rigorous workday." Restoring the sense of the cyclical is a way to induce certain detachment from the present and thus cope with the destruction of experience wrought by capitalism.

Between the Old and the New: Class, Gender and the Implosion of the Middle-Class Family

Peter Brooks (1976) and Thomas Elsaesser (1987) have traced the origins of the melodramatic form to the French Revolution. They explain that the highly codified (as through gesture, music and dialogue) and moralistic depictions of the innocent personality trapped amidst changing norms expressed the struggles of the bourgeois self caught between a nostalgia for the old and a search for the new. As Vasudevan (2011, 18) clarifies, the form was non-psychologized, that is, it was not so much about a person as about a personality whose innocence and suffering "framed a new world in which the personality emerged as the crucial vehicle of ethical and experiential truth." "The system of dramaturgy" in Hindi cinema, Vasudevan (1995, 307) elaborates, "is a melodramatic one, displaying the characteristic ensemble of Manichaeism, bipolarity, the privileging of the moral over the psychological, and the deployment of coincidence."

Taking the argument further, Vasudevan suggests that the distinguishing feature of melodrama in Hindi cinema is that individual travails within the family are tied to larger social and political changes. At the heart of contemporary Indian soaps are pure women who put convention above their own individual desires and survive a series of extreme trials and tribulations. What is also significant is that, in contrast to popular melodramatic films that overwhelmingly end with marriage, these soaps are obsessed with life after marriage. Their plots dwell on the conflicts between mothers- and daughters-in-law, the trials of good and virtuous couples, rivalries and jealousies within the extended family and the enduring bonds between mothers and daughters.

Sudhir and Katharina Kakkar (2007) noted that one of the most distinctive shifts in contemporary India is a move towards greater nuclearization, which is at least psychological, if not physical. At its core is, what the Kakkars call, the desire for the *Jodi* (couple), especially on the part of the young wife. The anguish born of the separation of Archana and Manav or Poorvi and Arjun clearly speaks to this desire as is the repeated conflict between living for oneself or others. Using direct address, which is now directed to the family, these soaps put their women characters on trial for failing or succeeding to reconcile the desire for coupledom with their roles in the family. Accordingly, Archana and her daughter, Poorvi, emerge as the ideals. They put the family first, but if required can take on a job and excel at it without competing with others. In fact, they treat their co-workers as family. These ideal women fit what Rittu Lukose (2009) has described as the "demure modern," that is, they are able to negotiate the binaries of the good and traditional versus the "modern," loose woman.

Daughters-in-law occupy a critical role in the transformation of the extended family and the public discourse around it. There is, on the one hand, as Nivedita Menon (2012) writes, an increasing refusal on the part of younger women to put up with the inherent violence of patriarchal *marriage* which requires women to leave their homes and move to the husband's or in-laws', change their names, and shift or obliterate their relationships and affections prior to marriage. Sudhir and Katharinia Kakkar (2007) take a slightly different tack, suggesting that rather than the implosion of marriage, what is going on is an increased push by the daughter-in-law for the recognition of the primacy of the marital bond over that of the role of daughter-in-law.

Well cognizant of the individuating effects of sexual attraction, the extended family, as the Kakkars note, built in stringent strictures against the unity of the couple superseding that of the family. These included the disapproval of any display of affection amongst the couple in public and bestowing special attention upon one's biological child – whose very existence indicates the sexual bond. These norms are being tested now and may be observed in increased expectations from marriage on the part of younger women. How to make marriages work is a popular topic amongst self-help books and they center on the conflict between meeting personal goals (or that of the couple) and family cohesion.[14]

Another aspect of the fragmentation of the middle-class family may be observed in a preoccupation in media as well as daily discourse with the loneliness, neglect and outright exploitation of the elderly. For instance, the parliament passed the Maintenance and Welfare of Parents and Senior Citizens Act in 2007, mandating children, grandchildren or others who might inherit wealth to take care of elderly parents or suffer a jail term of three months. This law makes children solely responsible for parents while the neoliberal economy undercuts both their ability and/or their inclination to do so. Continued economic uncertainty along with the ever-increasing lure of commodities on the market has increased children's dependence on parents both for their inheritance as well as their resources in the present. Meanwhile, the culture of radical individualism, which promotes self-care before all else, has radicalized the transformation of the parent-child relationship into an exchange relationship based on the market principles of cost-benefit analysis in which parental resources are coveted but parental care seen as a burden.

Ultimately, both forms of individuation within the family – whether enacted through the separation of the *Jodi* (couple) or children from parents – is stretching the bonds between generations. The open wound is then revisited every night on the flickering screens of television sets that hold up a mirror to the middle-class family, reassuring it that it's not alone in its fragmentation. The melodramatic plots urge self-regulation rather than transformation of external reality – because external reality is merely an illusion in a cycle without end. On the surface, these plots have strong moralistic overtones. Through the vicissitudes of their heroines' lives, they endlessly debate on the pros and cons of self-sacrifice. Yet, the endless recurrence of unresolved conflicts underlines the pointlessness of hoping for justice – a position which is, in the final analysis, amoral.

Capitalism – tied as it is to profits in the short term – blocks our ability to plan for the future, filling us with a dread of moving towards the future. However, living without hope is to live in an eternal present – a perception of the world that unites the pre-modern notion of the world itself as an illusion or *Maya* with the postmodern notion of reality as only a discourse. Yet, while the notion of *Maya* seeks to produce an "other" – centered orientation, neoliberalism turns inwards, producing a narcissistic obsession with self-invention. The former insists on ridding the self of the "illusion" of uniqueness. The latter, obsessively preoccupied with promoting and managing the self, also deepens the sense that the self is nothing but an idea. Both produce an experience of life as out of control, as if one is playing out a part in someone else's dream. It is the sort of dream where you wake up to find yourself in another dream.

Chapter 4

AN "ARRANGED LOVE" MARRIAGE: INDIA'S NEOLIBERAL TURN AND THE BOLLYWOOD WEDDING CULTURE INDUSTRY

Whether made in India or abroad, the big fat Bollywood wedding has become a trademark attraction of all that is Bollywood. A trend started by films such as *Hum Apke Hain Kaun…!* (Can You Name Our Relationship?) (Sooraj Barjatya 1994) and *Dilwale Dulhaniya Le Jayenge* (Those with Heart Will Take the Bride) (Aditya Chopra 1995), it has crossed over internationally via films such as, Mira Nair's *Monsoon Wedding* (2001) and Gurinder Chadha's *Bride and Prejudice* (2004). In turn, real weddings have become increasingly spectacular, egged on by a newly emerged wedding industry in which the Bollywood form has seamlessly merged. Celebrity weddings add fuel to the fire. Reportedly, British model Elizabeth Hurely's diamond encrusted wedding sari cost £4,000 while the tiny gold balls dangling from leading film star Aishwarya Rai's wedding sari were – in the tradition of the maharajas – distributed to the "poor."[1] In a perceptive review of Mira Nair's *Namesake* (2007), Stuart Klawans (2007) commended Nair for directing the film, particularly the wedding scenes, with "the instincts of a hostess" – a comparison which indicates the extent to which staging a wedding as a cinematic attraction has blurred into staging its real counterpart as a film-in-the-making.

How might we understand this reinvention of tradition at the very moment India is supposed to have broken from history to emerge as a power in the global economy, this assertion of ethnic identity in the midst of an unprecedented presence of global brands and the "discovery" of Indian cinema, specifically Bollywood, as a national icon at the height of its global fame? It will be my argument that the Bollywood wedding is a specific class-based, gendered response to India's turn to neoliberalism. In other words, the meta-narratives of capital and patriarchy can explain what on the surface appears to be a paradoxical or free-wheeling postmodern intermingling of opposites or differences. The big Bollywood wedding – its conspicuous consumption dictated by the need to individuate oneself, to package and present oneself as a globalized Indian who flamboyantly embraces "tradition" as a matter of choice – is symptomatic of a neoliberal subject governed by a regime of consumption where, in order to show that one has "arrived," every event, including something as conformist as a wedding, must be presented as uniquely individual.

At the outset, it is important to clarify that I am not using the term Bollywood, as it is often done in popular discourse, to refer to the entire gamut of Indian popular cinema. Rather, following Ashis Rajadhyaksha (2003, 37), I use it specifically to describe a particular genre of glossy, nationalistic, family-oriented "'feel-good' version of 'our culture' films centered on romantic stories" which emerged in the 1990s and crossed over into North America and the UK to become the cultural icons of a globalizing India. This genre is at the heart of what can quite appropriately be called the Bollywood culture industry – marketing a cultural style that extends beyond cinema to an entire range of cultural production, across media like video, television and print to lifestyle markers such as fashion, food and decor. Promoted by both the Indian government and business, its basic commodity and brand is a playful postmodern reinvention of "Indian culture" that is built around recycling familiar orientalist tropes within an extravaganza of consumer culture. The sparkle and glitter of Bollywood projects a world of affluence that is free of work but filled with pleasurable comingling with others. For instance, the New York Association of American Advertisers hosted the Bollywood Ball in 2007 at the luxury hotel, the Pierre in Manhattan (a new acquisition by the Indian multinational Tata Group), setting it up with such "trendy Bollywood" delights as hookahs, henna and palm readers. The "India Everywhere" campaign launched by the Confederation of Indian Industry and the Indian government at the World Economic Forum, Davos in 2006, earned the following praise from the magazine *India Today* (Purie 2006):

> The difference with earlier attempts to promote India was stark. This time, it was Bollywood music and spicy food, a clear signal that India needed to, and was, changing its act and presenting the modern face of the country.

In other words, Bollywood is culture indistinguishable from commerce. It is the unabashed connection with money that jazzes up "tradition" making it fashionable to be Indian once again. In this sense, the term culture industry – evocative of the Frankfurt school – is particularly apt for Bollywood. It helps see cultural production both as a means of generating surplus value as well as subjectivities amenable to capitalism.

But first, a description of the phenomenon itself. The wedding, more specifically the Hindu wedding, has become a significant addition to the attractions of popular Hindi cinema, fitting easily into an aesthetic (Gopalan 2002) and a mode of production (Pendakur 2003; Prasad 1998), that foregrounds itself as an assembly of attractions and its narratives – not driven by the classical Hollywood paradigm of deadlines – stop for popular elements such as the "item number" or the "fight sequence." The Bollywood film has, however, taken this form and subjected it to what Rustom Bharucha (1995) calls a "ruthless" and "claustrophobic" leveling of narrative and dramatic possibilities. These films, according to Bharucha, have no arch-villains, antagonisms, conflicts or the moral universe of the Hindi film in which the battle between right and wrong is played out with intense emotional melodrama. He may well be speaking of wedding films such as *Vivah* (Wedding) (Barjatiya et al. 2006), *Mujh Se Shaadi Karogi* (Will You Marry Me?) (Bazmee et al. 2004), *Kal Ho Naa Ho* (Tomorrow May or May Not Be) (Iyengar 2003), *Kabhi Khushi Kabhi Gham* (Sometimes Happiness Sometimes Sorrow) (Johar and Parikh 2001), *Mere Yaar Ki Shaadi Hain* (My Friend's Wedding) (Gadhvi and Puri 2002) and *Kuch Kuch Hota Hai* (There's That Certain Feeling) (Johar 1998). The key goal in all these films is to get the protagonists married to those they desire with the full participation of their families. The participation of the families is garnered through the celebration of various traditional rituals, some of them invented.

Vivah, the most conservative in this set, narrated the romance and trials of a young couple as they advance from an arranged marriage to the wedding itself. The plot stretches into a three-hour celebration of the various steps involved in arranging a wedding, presenting the traditional wedding as a pure and innocent act of faith between two families and individuals. While *Vivah* was set in a small-town, *Mere Yaar Ki Shaadi Hain* had a more contemporary, urban setting. The film was loosely based on the American film *My Best Friend's Wedding* (P. J. Hogan 1997), except in this case it was the man who realized his desire for his friend at her wedding and he gets her in the end. Along the way to its resolution, the film lingers on various wedding ceremonies, including an affluent bachelor's party – replete with disco lights, costumes and unabashed sexualized innuendo. In *Kuch Kuch Hota Hai*, an eight-year-old plots to get her widowed father married to his old college friend who is by now engaged to someone else, so we get to see her engagement with one and her lavish wedding with another. The child's desire to see her father remarried – upon the urging of her dead mother, of course – anchors the film and grants it an emotional tenor. The protagonist of *Kal Ho Na Ho* – upon realizing that he has a fatal form of cancer – sets about making the woman he loves fall in love with and marry another. The wedding here takes place in New York and the attraction is the successful Indian community in the city. *Kabhi Khushi Kabhi Gham* – a movie about the separation and final reconciliation of a father and son on account of the son's refusal to marry the woman chosen by his father – nevertheless throws in a lavish wedding and a *kurva-chauth* (ritual fast undertaken by wives for the well-being of their husbands).

Even more than cinema, television soaps revel in the cult of the wedding, celebrating it with daily regularity and sometimes inventing rituals and resuscitating others better forgotten – such as *jamai puja* (son-in-law worship) or *muh dikhai* (seeing the bride for the first time). Shows that are set in large extended families like *Teen Bahuraniya* (Three Daughters-in-Law) (Joshi et al. 2007), *Ghar Ki Beti Lakshmiya Betiyann* (Daughters Are Goddesses Lakshmi) (Creative Eye Limited 2006), *Kasam Se* (I Promise) (Nim Sood et al. 2006), *Maayka* (Mother's Home) (Mrinal Jha and Brij Mohan 2007) and *Saat Phere* (The Seven Steps [of the Hindu wedding]) (Rajesh Dubey and Purnendu Shekhar 2005) punctuate their already loose plots with celebrations of the married couple around festivals and seasons all year long, often in synch with the actual festivals. These television families constantly remind viewers of the numerous festivals that mark the traditional Hindu calendar, celebrating them in grand style in homes that come equipped with alters that would outdo many public temples. Domestic space in these serials is thus colonized by religious symbols, predominantly Hindu, against which these television families enact their internal dramas, both big and small. Organizing private spaces around religion in this way inscribes religious or caste identities as primary.

Real weddings, in turn, are Bollywoodized, enacting and inventing rituals mediated by media and advertising. For instance, wedding sites, such as IndianWeddingSite.com, encourage their clients to view Bollywood films for inspiration, including designing outfits, staging festivities, and choreographing dance numbers. Wedding planners and coordinators, like Regal-Weddings.com, offer wedding packages evocative of Bollywood plots, such as this ad for a stage-managed elopement from a feudal-era building, all made possible by modern conveniences such as hotels and airports:

> Mandawa is a beautiful market town of the colorful Shekhawati region. It is famous for the castle now converted into a heritage hotel & the fresco paintings. One can plan an elope from the hustle of city life to get married in a Village setting. Closest Airport is Jaipur.

For the transnational class, whose eyes are turned outwards, the marriage between tradition and modern conveniences is clinched by international brand recognition. In the following ad, the approval of the *Brides* magazine confers distinction, to use Bourdieu's term (1984), to the "world class Indian consumer":

> Devigarh Fort Palace is located 27 Kms away from Udaipur. *Brides* has recommended Devigarh for an exotic and lavish Wedding. Witnessing the changes for more than two centuries stands the Devigarh Palace echoing memories of the Royal past [*sic*].

Then, there is the out-and-out Bollywood wedding. Planners suggest entire weddings around a Bollywood theme, such as a star or a movie. For the ultimate spectacle and those with deep pockets, a film star may perform at a wedding. Shah Rukh Khan, the reigning male star, is known to charge $15,000 for a two-hour appearance and $13 million for a dance number (eight crore rupees in current exchange rates) (Soumyadipta Banerjee 2013). Bollywood not only sets fashions, trends and expectations, it is also in the direct business of spin-offs. For example, Tanishq, a jewelry brand owned by the Tatas (known for their cars), launched its "Paheli Collection" alongside the film *Paheli* (Amol Palekar 2005). This was, perhaps, the first film in which the jewelry had its own credit line. Right after the opening credits appears the inter-title "Jewellery designed by Tanishq."

Bollywood has also entered the wedding business more directly. Ramoji Film City has a wedding wing that serves as a "one stop shop" for all aspects of wedding planning. From designing sets to offering entertainment and hospitality, including putting up guests and driving them around, the studio can also perform the wedding ceremony itself. Wedding-Regal advertises:

> You can choose from a variety of magical venues for your wedding, each unique and breathtakingly beautiful. Whatever the settings, we ensure to make your wedding a dream wedding – Perfect to the last detail. Choose from these spectacular wedding venues […] Taj Mahal, Mayfair, Pool Side, Lake View Garden, Moghul Garden, Sun Fountain, Leg Garden, Dream Valley, Majestic Garden, Sierra Garden, Eureka Entry Plaza, Eureka Central Court, Princess Street, B. S. F. Halls, Terrace Hall or a bus stop.

Not only does the studio offer to organize the mise-en-scène it also promises to film the wedding in a way that would out-do Bollywood itself:

> With the world's largest film studio, expert photographers and complete film crew at your disposal, make the silver screen weddings look pale in front of yours. (Ramoji Film City n.d.)

For those who may want a more non-mainstream approach, there is the documentary-style video offered by Anoli Patel, whose production company, *Shaadi Story* (Wedding Story), also directed the Discovery Channel's series on Indian weddings. Each wedding film costs $20,000–50,000 and justifies its price on the claim that each film is an artistic project that rejects formulaic Bollywood style to show the uniqueness of each wedding. The filmmakers weave in interviews with relatives and also perform re-enactments such as taking the couple to the college where they first met (Nirali Magazine 2007).

In keeping with the hyper-spectacular neoliberal economy, the wedding industry has brought in new occupations unknown prior to the '90s. Incorporating what was previously part of an informal economy or a familial ethic, wedding planners and professional DJs have replaced the experienced family relative and the filmy aunt or uncle who entertained everyone. Other jobs have become professionalized and specialized – photography, catering, wedding cards, decorations, beauticians and henna artists and entertainers. It is this industry which has brought us excesses, such as dessert menus with forty choices, decorations including orchids flown from Thailand, brides making entries through diaphanous moons and entertainment provided by Spanish flamenco dancers or belly dancers. According to a report (A. Das, 2005), the minimum budget for a middle-class wedding is now $34,000 while the upper-middle and rich classes are known to spend upwards of $2 million, not including cash and valuables given as part of a dowry. Spin-offs of this industry have included discounts by Samsung, Sony, LG and other appliance makers during the wedding season, "auspicious" personal loans offered by GE Money India and wedding malls and bridal exhibitions held in India and abroad.

To be clear, weddings in India have always been major affairs, celebrated as crucial events in an individual's and family's life. They establish class status, ensure that property is passed along patriarchal lines in the form of dowry – typically given by the bride's family to the groom's – and indicate the end of the daughter's rights over the assets of her parental home. The wedding seals heterosexuality and sets up marriage – and with it sexuality as well as raising children within the patriarchal family – as a highly desirable social goal. The confluence between at least one aspect of Hindi cinema – that is, the film song and the wedding – is not new either. The relationship is mutual and circular – film songs draw upon folk songs sung at weddings and in turn are easily assimilated into the repertoire of wedding songs.

What is new, however, is the transformation of the wedding into an expression of personal style and the ostentatious display of wealth that has accompanied it – an unabashed departure from an earlier Gandhian-Nehruvian embarrassment around conspicuous consumption in a predominantly poor nation. Bollywood has played an important ideological role in validating this move. The incessant replays of spectacular weddings and happy playful families celebrating traditional rituals in plush homes has turned, as Patricia Uberoi (2006) and Rustom Bharucha (1995) discuss, affluence into a traditional and even spiritual value. These Bollywood families are blissfully free of financial worries – middle-class fathers in films such as *Hum Aapke Hain Kaun...!* and *Vivah* marry off their daughters to the wealthiest households with fanfare served by happy servants dressed in ethnic chic. It is a harmonious world where dowries are gladly given but not taken. In *Hum Aapke Hain Kaun...!* the bride's father offers a "TV set, diamond jewelry, an imported car and a VCR" but the groom's family refuses to take them because, as the patriarch of the groom's family declares, they came nowhere near the real "wealth" they are taking with them, that is, the daughter-in-law.

The dowry list recounted in *Hum Apke Hain Kaun...!* recites items which had become standard in the eighties – a period during which the then prime minister, Rajiv Gandhi, started to relax restrictions on consumer goods, enabling the middle class, keen on consumption (Varma 1999), to acquire these items. Rajiv Gandhi's government lowered taxes on imports, particularly automobiles and goods previously characterized as luxury items, such as color televisions and refrigerators. It was this period which saw a substantive increase in dowry demands and its accompanying practice of in-laws harassing young women for dowry even after the marriage. In its most brutal form, the harassment culminated in the murder or suicide of young women in their marital homes. For my generation, who entered college in the early '80s – and particularly those of us who were radicalized in the Marxist-feminist movement – the big wedding was repugnant, the very opposite of romance. It enacted women's humiliation as property and a means of acquiring more property.[2] Consequently for us, rejecting the traditional wedding in favor of a civil ceremony or rejecting marriage in its entirety was the way to assert individual autonomy and an expression of authentic commitment.

This then brings us to what is truly new about the contemporary big wedding phenomenon. It is an ongoing invention of tradition that is driven by and representative of neoliberal subjectivity. The neoliberal subject is a product of the free market insistence on privatization of resources and its concomitant ethic that the individual expresses her or his identity through choices made in the market. These market-produced choices become means to invent, package, and present oneself, thus driving and being driven by a market of consumer goods that is relentless in its pursuit of novelty. Thus, "tradition" is invented – an irony encapsulated in the oxymoron: a "traditional designer wedding."

The lead in designing these "traditions" is taken, not by the grandmothers and the grandfathers, but by the brides and the grooms who are shouldering the burdens of organizing these weddings that, for most, still have to be done within a budget. Designing one's own wedding – that is, expecting to make it uniquely reflective of one's personality – is, in fact, entirely incompatible with a traditional orientation. The wedding marks an individual's entrance into, not separation from, the social. For the young men and women – in particular those from the middle class – who fancy such assertion of individuality it involves a great deal of work. Recognizing the work it takes to put up a wedding, online wedding magazines like Nirali follow up the to-do lists with sanctimonious advice to not get flustered and to remember "to bask" in your special day. The sheer conformity and work involved in consumption is passed off as a matter of choice and self-expression.

The neoliberal subject is regulated not by covert force but by stress, the stress of asserting individuality and style, through the consumption of market-produced goods – goods that, for the middle class, can be acquired only through a relentless regimen of work and earning money. The power of the wedding, however, is that it anchors the hollowness of relentlessly reinventing oneself into family and community, saving it, perhaps, from the vacuous wanderings of the postmodern subject of advanced capitalism. Yet, this grounding re-inscribes the hierarchies of caste and class, gender and heterosexuality. The wedding is a prime example of an institution that sutures the atomized, self-regulating individual into social hierarchies and ties work to purchasing power.

As elsewhere, the market has granted certain recognition to women and the young on account of their invention as consumers. Women are invited to treat themselves to cosmetics and cars, and this ethos of autonomy has also generated fears and panics around the sexual autonomy of women. The big wedding is a happy resolution – the threat of unbridled sexuality is domesticated by marriage, with the wedding itself acting as a kind of carnivalesque play of sexuality. Borrowing from folk tradition, the songs in these wedding films are bawdy, allude to sexual relations between in-laws, such as brothers-in-laws and sister-in-laws, and express a raucous appreciation of sexuality. Yet, at the same time, these films go to great lengths to advertise themselves as "clean, healthy family" entertainment as opposed to the broader sexualization of consumer culture, which is seen as an undesirable side effect of economic deregulation. The songs, Uberoi (2006) writes, are "sanitized" and order is restored as the bride is sent off to her marital home with everyone appropriately in tears.

In *Hum Aapke Hain Kaun....!*, when the protagonist is asked what kind of marriage he would like – an arranged marriage or a love marriage – he replies, without a moment of hesitation, an "arranged love marriage."

The pact between patriarchy and capital – the limited opening up of sexuality by consumer culture and its containment within patriarchy – could not have been expressed in a pithier phrase than this one. The "arranged love marriage" is a match between families of equal social status where sexuality is sublimated in the acquisition of goods and the maintenance of traditional hierarchies, where free market meets the hierarchies of caste, class and gender and where all contradictions of capital are happily resolved by a voluntary return to patriarchal tradition.

   Women are prepared for such an arrangement through numerous calls to combine the traditional with the modern, the ethnic with the global. What follows is an example, a kind of fashion manifesto for the "girl next door," that appeared in *Femina*, a women's magazine:

> The girl next door will be the intelligent one. Completely shunning any fashion in any form, she will find the balance between respect for the ethnic, a touch of adventure, technological development and vintage rag-picking. The message will be clear. I picked this myself. I put it together myself. I dress for myself. Her USP [Unique Selling Point] will be a connection forged between opposites. Indian values/international value, distilled to perfection. From her spray on lip gloss to smudged on kohl, expect the new citizen of the world. (In Rodricks 2007, 88)

Some have seen this mixing of tradition and modernity as an example of hybridity, a notion that has gained much currency in explanations of the cultural changes that have accompanied the late twentieth-century wave of capitalist globalization. According to Sumita Chakravarty, *Hum Aapke Hain Kaun…!* (in spite of its consumerist values) "reversed the effects of the global invasion on our culture, implicitly asserting the permanence and stability of all institutions of our traditional culture that are now under severe threat – the joint family, patriarchy, the traditional qualities of the image of the Indian woman, and also, the nation."[3] For Sheila Nayar, the emphasis on family and tradition in Indian cinema serves to successfully diffuse *"all tension between oneself and one's immediate family, and between one's immediate family and one's future spouse"* (1996, 86; original emphasis). Faiza Hirji (2005) sums it up:

> Bollywood has managed to arrive at a compromise that allows it to assert and affirm traditional values for fans within India and across the diasporic community without becoming mired in what seems like an increasingly *fruitless* [emphasis added] attempt to deny the significance of all-pervasive symbols of Westernization.

The central opposition here is assumed to be that between "Western" culture and "ours," with ours represented by family and tradition, imagined as free of any internal conflicts – of class, caste or gender – and resilient enough to absorb the threats of the former which is also imagined as a homogenized bloc. This reasserts a form of cultural nationalism where the nation becomes increasingly identified with Hinduism.

The notion of hybridity, as proposed by postcolonial theory also echoes this "nationalist" view although its main thrust appears not so much to assert the cultural superiority of Indian tradition as to insist on the inability of capitalist hegemony to subsume all that stands in its way. Critiquing the Frankfurt school and the Cultural Imperialism thesis for their "totalization narratives" of an overall homogenization of culture under the regime of capitalist consumer culture, William Mazzarella (2003, 37) advances Homi Bhabha's (1990) notion of "third space" and Dipesh Chakrabarty's "generative gap" at the heart of the commodity (in Mazarella 2003, 38). Both reassert that capital can never completely control the meanings generated by the commodity. If this were the case, Mazzarella quotes Chakrabarty, "there would be no room for enjoyment in the rule of capital, no play of desires, no seduction of the commodity" (20). Bhabha's (1990) ode to cultural hybridity reads like a MasterCard or Visa advertisement, promising seamless access to the goods and experiences of the world to the discerning world traveler:

> America leads to Africa; the notions of Europe and Asia meet in Australia; the margins of the nation displace the center [...] the great Whitmanesque sensorium of America is exchanged for a Warhol blowup, a Kruger installation, or Mapplethorpe's naked bodies. (6)

Drawing upon the postcolonial notion of hybridity, Marwan Kraidy (1999, 472), among others, has advocated the term "glocalization" to help reformulate "intercultural and international communication beyond buoyant models of resistance and inauspicious patterns of domination." Faiza Hijiri quotes Nasreen Kabir (1999) in support of her argument about the "glocal" moves of popular Hindi cinema:

> Western culture and glitter are very attractive. So *Maine Pyar Kiya* and *Hum Aapke Hain Kaun....!* offer the solution: a happy marriage between the two worlds. I can have everything offered by modernisation, and still hold on to family values and tradition at the same time. (Kabir 1999, 95)

In this discourse, even popular Bombay cinema – that industrialized media industry driven by profit – has come to stand for some innate Indian-ness, a forum for defense against modernity (not capitalism). Ashis Nandy (1983, 235) elaborates:

> [...] when much of the oppression and violence in society is inflicted in the name of categories such as development, science, progress, and national security, there has grown a tacit demand for a different kind of political attitude towards cultural traditions. However much we may bemoan the encroachment of mass culture through the commercial cinema, the fact remains that it is commercial cinema which, if only by default, has been more responsive to such demands and more protective towards nonmodern categories.

These "nonmodern" categories or the "innocence" with which Indians met Western colonialism is for Nandy (1983, ix, 108) the innate Indian ability "to live with cultural ambiguities and to use them to build psychological and even metaphysical defences against cultural invasions" (108). Popular Indian cinema, for Nandy, then "creates a space for the global, the unitary and the homogenizing, but does so in terms of a principle of plurality grounded in traditions" (1995, 13). The plurality of tradition that Nandy sees in Indian cinema reinforces religious and/or ethnic identity as the primary identity.

Drawing upon poststructuralism and its disavowal of universals, postcolonial theory can, and does, turn into a culturalism that, Sumit Sarkar (1997) and Aijaz Ahmed (1995) explain, divorces itself from any consideration of political-economic formation and therefore can paradoxically celebrate both hybridity and cultural specificity. More specifically, in terms of the discussion at hand, if on the one hand the Bollywood wedding can be seen as an expression of hybridity or cultural negotiation, it can equally be held up as an instance of cultural assertion against foreign cultural invasion unless one brings into the discussion the meta-narratives of capitalism and patriarchy. After all, whether performed as a consumerist extravagant designer wedding or an "arranged love marriage," the Bollywood wedding's reinvention of "tradition" can easily be appropriated into the religious nationalist project of retaining privilege and wealth in class- and caste-based patriarchal households. Stated differently, the religious fundamentalist project is a modern phenomenon. It seeks to create something new – only the new looks towards the past and, therefore, is a reactionary response to the present. So long as we use the term "modernity" and not "capitalism," we remain bound to the limits of the paradox inherent in the use of "modernity" – where societies co-existing on the same planet are presumed to be non-contemporaneous, as in the distinction established between modern and pre-modern.

Ultimately, the Bollywood wedding culture industry is grounded in the contradictions confronting the Indian middle class: it must assert its membership in a transnational bourgeoisie while retaining patriarchal and caste based hierarchies at home. Reinventing tradition as a way to assert cultural superiority, Sumit Sarkar (1997, 107) clarifies, is not new to middle-class formation – the propensity to combine "material advancement" with "spiritual autonomy" was common amongst the colonial middle class in the nineteenth and early twentieth centuries, particularly for those upwardly mobile sections who benefitted from collaboration with colonialism. Then, as now, Tanika Sarkar (2001) adds, it created a way to come to terms with dependency by asserting cultural or religious superiority – an assertion that was premised upon the celebration of home and women as a pure and private sphere. This comingling of economic submission to global capital and assertion of cultural superiority is now resurrected in the celebration of the large affluent Hindu, joint family home as a private temple where Indian tradition and culture remains thriving and unchanged – the family a "portable institution" (Uberoi 2006, 183) which can exist anywhere or simultaneously in several places on the globe. Affluent homes, weddings and traditional rituals provide the mise-en-scène for validating the culture of spending and high living, a fantastic backdrop which serves as an object lesson in consumerism for the middle class – the poster-child of neoliberalism.

Consumption is, in capitalism, primarily a private affair – after all, one's ability to buy depends on the depth of one's pocket. Under neoliberalism, economic growth is measured in terms of the increase in private consumption – a switch, that Leela Fernandes (2006) indicates, has transformed citizenship into acts of consumption such as the acquisition of laptops, cars, cosmetics, mobile phones and CEO lifestyles. In order to accumulate profit, capitalism must incessantly privatize spaces of consumption by eroding the socialized spaces of consumption such as public health, education or transport. The new architecture of neoliberalism, including its imaginary spaces, is driven by the necessity of producing exclusive and guarded spaces where image and reality, commodity and spectacle, can constantly feed into each other. The spectacular wedding, both real and imagined, is but a symptom in such a trajectory of privatization which includes the air-conditioned mall and the five-star hotel policed by private security guards and surveillance cameras.

The obstruction in the path of neoliberalism is exactly this contradiction; private consumption has to occur in heavily guarded private enclaves guarded by the very class which is a threat to such consumption. The alarm bells were recently sounded by none other than the current prime minister, Manmohan Singh, the man under whose leadership as finance minister the "reforms" were initiated in 1991. Singh called for restraint in the "vulgar display of wealth" around weddings that, according to him, "insult the poverty of the less privileged, [are] socially wasteful, and plants seeds of resentment in the minds of the have-nots."[4] Of course, he was condemning the vulgarity of the *display* of wealth and not the wealth itself or its defense by equally vulgar displays of power. Private armed guards are fast becoming a regular feature of upper-middle-class weddings and even birthday parties. The cruel irony and flammable spark latent in a lavish wedding, supposedly a celebration of the union of two individuals and families, guarded by an armed underclass is not an example of hybridity but a contradiction – an explicit manifestation of the unstable foundations of capitalism.

It is true, as Mazzarella and Chakrabarty claim, that capital cannot absorb all desires within it, that the commodity form has contradictory possibilities that escape and even go beyond existing hierarchies. However, ascribing possibilities to the commodity form sounds remarkably similar to the discourse of aspirations so loved by the advertisers and marketers. It neglects to consider that the possibilities of the commodity are tied to one's purchasing power. Capitalism makes life appear accidental, dangerous and, imprisoned as it is in competition and acquisition, ultimately out of control. It crushes one of the deepest quests of human life that is, to find the meaning of the fragile, beautiful and mysterious entity we know as our individual life and to reconcile that personal experience with death. Such reconciliation rests upon a return to human society not a separation from it. We experience such restoration when our own time is sutured in natural time; our own lives seem part of the river of life or time. "What we have called love," writes Terry Eagleton (2007, 97), "is the way we can reconcile our search for individual fulfillment with the fact that we are social animals." Here Eagleton reiterates a fundamental Marxist assertion: "To be individuated is an activity of our species being, not a condition at odds with it" (96). It is this defining feature of our humanity that gives us the ability to belong to culture. We articulate our own individuality in language, but our ability to speak rests upon our being human.

Perhaps somewhere in these big weddings lies a yearning for another sense of time, one which restores the individual to the social and the everyday to the natural. The wedding offers a reprieve from the capitalist logic of using time to accumulate and, instead, ushers in a reminder of the recurrence of seasons, life and death, and thus reconciles generations and the individual to the human community. The several days of merrymaking that precede the wedding and the carnivalesque obsession with sexuality and food serve to convince – especially the middle class or "aspirationals" as they are called in marketing lingo – that there is a payoff to the relentless time-discipline required of surviving in the new economy. For the wedding, time is taken off from work – a luxury not allowed before or after it. Marriage self-help books wring their hands over the stresses on marriage as time is drowned in marking off achievements on checklists in a world where there are no guarantees, only endless change. The Bollywood wedding, much like the return to the *Mahabharata* discussed earlier, is a specific class response of the middle class to the anxieties of radicalized capitalism. It packages the yearning to come to terms with the limitations of one's own finite lifetime into one garish display of the utmost conformism – where the self disappears rather than asserts its autonomy.

To end this chapter, I offer the following subversive wedding card comparing arranged marriages and love marriages. Here the wedding is cut off from commodity culture, the assertion of status, and the accumulation of debt and is turned into a celebration of individuals committing to one another in love.

Figure 15. The arranged marriage costs are as follows: Rs. 2 lakhs[5] on the wedding, 4 lakhs on jewelry and 0.5 lakhs on rituals. Total for three days: Rs. 6.5 lakhs, or Rs. 216,666.66 per day. The love marriage costs are as follows: Rs. 100 for the stamp form, 20 for the notary and 50 for the photo. Total: Rs. 220. "Your money, your desire and your own decision. Wake up customers! Escape with your lovers!"

Chapter 5

EK HASEENAH THI (THERE ONCE WAS A MAIDEN): THE VANISHING MIDDLE CLASS AND OTHER NEOLIBERAL THRILLS

Escape routine. Escape mundane. Escape usual. These 2–3 bedroom apartments with fitted modular kitchen and air conditioning in every room are specially designed to keep the world outdoors. You can hear your own body pumping, gurgling, and finally drifting off to sleep under a star clad universe when the world is whispering… in awe of your escape.[1]

The above quote from a burgeoning industry in housing in gated communities evocatively captures the narcissism of buying one's way out of the sharpening inequalities that have accompanied India's turn to neoliberalism. With names such as Hamilton Court, Regency Park, Windsor Manor, Malibu Towne, Beverly Hills, Orange County, Boulder Hill, Sierra or Hiranandani Chelsea, these privatized enclosures are concrete manifestations of the desire to escape the world that lies just outside their walls. But, as the ad clarifies, the pleasure of the escape rests upon the envy of others left far below.

These high-rises stand out as sparkling lighthouses in a sea of darkness when routine power outages submerge the surrounding areas in darkness. Security guards, surveillance cameras and identity checks jealously guard these private enclosures, including their own schools, playgrounds, walking paths and health spas. Accompanying this privatization of living space is a culture of consumption equally walled and guarded in malls and multiplexes. Air-conditioned and heavily guarded by armed guards and security cameras, these shopping spaces create a sterile, heavily controlled comfort zone within which the new and the strange may be sold as an object, an experience or an image. Together, they form the new architecture of neoliberalism.

In this very decade and a half following the policies of "structural adjustment," a new genre has appeared in Hindi cinema playing to niche multiplex audiences. This is the conspiracy thriller set in the new urban spaces of neoliberal India. Like the Hollywood conspiracy film, the protagonist finds her or himself framed by a powerful antagonist, either known or unknown to them, and compelled to undertake tasks in which the stakes are high, involving their lives, the lives of loved ones or the lives of strangers. Fredric Jameson (1992; 1998) has described the conspiracy genre as a "poor person's mapping of the postmodern age," the response of an imaginary that is befuddled by the "social totality that is global capitalism" and unable to grasp its complex interconnections (1998, 356).[2] The protagonists of the conspiracy thriller, Jameson suggests, find themselves like postmodern subjects in a complex global world that seems infinitely fragmented on the surface but interconnected underneath – in other words, trapped in a larger system of relations and events that are beyond their control. Yet, the very survival of these protagonists depends upon uncovering the system of relations and the interconnections between events, and they must do so just in nick of time. These narratives express the deepening experience of contemporary life as profoundly networked. Economic crises such as falling house prices and rising gas prices produce unemployment and loss of homes; global war and terrorism make daily life increasingly uncertain; 24/7 work in a global economy and the easy mobility of digital technologies produce a sense of powerlessness in having to depend upon unknown others. What does the appearance of this genre in contemporary India tell us about the nature of subjectivities engendered by neoliberalism, particularly the experience of time?

The answer, in my view, lies both in the texts and the contexts of their exhibition. Playing to niche multiplex audiences in spaces opened up by neoliberalism itself, the thriller is both a product and a symptom of neoliberalism and can offer some key insights into subjectivities engendered by it. In particular, the genre in India seems preoccupied with anxieties around the loss of class privilege as the middle-class protagonists – steadily stripped of their wealth of connections – start to descend into the abyss of a nameless crowd where survival depends upon the sheer speed with which dangers are met, the new communication technologies used and the spaces traversed. Time and space become separated as the individual must "read" and consume space rather than occupy it and so, place becomes subservient to time. The body is literally an obstruction as it is reduced to keeping pace with externally imposed deadlines. Thus, poised between the First and Third Worlds – both separating rapidly in contemporary India – the protagonist enacts the steady erosion of the Second World, the routine-bound, cautious and comfortable world of the salaried middle class which has accompanied the policy of structural adjustment.

When experienced within the protected enclave of the multiplex and the mall, the adventures of the protagonist offer this terrifying new uncertainty as a thrill – much like other virtual experiences of speed that have become part of contemporary urban living, in particular the speed with which distances can be smashed through new communication technologies. Ironically, it is the documentary or reality footage of the world outside the mall that offers this thrill – that is, reality turned into a spectacle for those who live as tourists or detectives in their home cities or bodies.

In this chapter, I wish to discuss the nuances of this generic representation through a close reading of *Ek Haseenah Thi* (There Once Was a Maiden) (Raghavan and Surti 2004). However, it is important to note that the film is part of a trend with plots often directly lifted from world cinemas. For instance, *Ek Din 24 Ghante* (One Day 24 Hours) (Balani 2003), partly reminiscent of *Run Lola Run* (Tom Tykwer 1998, Germany), narrates the story of a young woman who must release her boyfriend from the gangster who is holding him by delivering a large ransom. At the end of her rescue, however, she learns that she had, all along, been set up by her boyfriend – someone her wayward, estranged father had derided all along as a good-for-nothing. Her trust in her boyfriend is shattered and along with it descends a dawning sense of the futility to escape corruption, deceit or lies.

Aamir (Raj Kumar Gupta 2008) recounts the trials of a young Muslim doctor who, upon his return from London, finds himself trapped in a terrorist plot that requires him to set off a bomb in order to save his family. The mastermind behind the conspiracy sends Aamir on a journey through the city's poorest Muslim ghettos. This journey is meant to drive home the lesson that Aamir's pride in his personal achievements and belief in freedom of choice are misguided illusions born of a misplaced faith in the Indian republic by the upwardly mobile Muslim, who must also delink himself from the rest of his own Muslim community trapped in cycles of poverty. Over the course of the day, Aamir encounters the Third World in India, going through narrow lanes, filthy bathrooms and streets – some of which, shot with hidden cameras, give the film a startlingly realist effect. In the end, Aamir chooses to die with the bomb rather than blow up others, thus sacrificing himself and also possibly his family. In contrast to *Ek Din 24 Ghante*, *Aamir* suggests that it is possible for an individual to act and assert choice. However, it underlies this validation of individual action with a profound recognition of the over-determined nature of individual action in contemporary India. The only way in which Aamir can affirm his individuality is by choosing death. Recognizing that he has the bomb on his person and looking into the eyes of the potential victim, a child, Aamir chooses his own death over the others on the bus. However, this act of courage is tragically drowned in the hegemonic cacophony of the age – the news broadcasts that follow identify Aamir as a terrorist who had apparently lost his nerve just before setting off the bomb.

Unlike *Kahaani* – discussed earlier in this book – *Aamir* does not succumb to moral relativism and the meaninglessness of individual action; rather it is a tribute to the desire to live authentically. The choice of death in this case is an assertion of freedom against the meaninglessness imposed on individuals when forced into predetermined slots.

In *Deadline: Sirf 24 Ghante* (Deadline 24 Hours) (Khan and Shukla 2006), loosely based on *Trapped* (Luis Mandoki 2002, US), a wealthy doctor's child is kidnapped by three co-conspirators for a high ransom to be paid within 24 hours. Beginning with sympathy for the doctor and his family, the film ends in a twist that takes the film in a very different direction from the American one. It turns out that the kidnappers were, in fact, victims of the doctor's ambition and greed. They are the very middle-class parents and uncle of a child who had died because the doctor had refused to operate on him until his fees were paid in full. The father is a journalist and the mother an actor, both part of a professional intelligentsia that formed the backbone of India's post-1947 urban middle-class – a class that idealized its profession as a reward in itself and not as a means to make money or acquire fame. The kidnapping in this film then turns out to be a lesson against greed for money and fame, reminding the doctor of the real purpose of his profession, that is, to save lives. In the course of securing the release of his daughter from her kidnappers he realizes the real value of a human life.

In *Naqaab* (Shiraz Ahmed et al. 2007), almost a literal copy of *Dot the I* (Matthew Parkhill 2003, Spain), a filmmaker sets up a plot to make a "reality" film without telling his protagonists that they are actors in his film. He strikes a relationship with a young woman, proposes marriage to her, and then sets up another actor to seduce her away from the wedding. The actor and the woman end up falling in love and learn, much to their shock, that they were both set up – with the most intimate scenes of the relationship recorded by hidden cameras. Ultimately, the lovers get their revenge on the filmmaker, murdering him and, getting away with it, turn his own tactical blurring of film and reality against him. The ethical dilemma of using the other for money or success is very much at the heart of this film as well. The woman is portrayed as working-class (flouting realism in the nature of Bombay popular cinema, she flips burgers in Burger King and insists on paying rent to the extravagantly wealthy filmmaker when she lives with him) while the actor is shown struggling for work. In contrast to the other films mentioned above, the spaces in this one are entirely fictional, set in the glamour world of the super wealthy film festivals and hotels – without any of the documentary footage characteristic of the former. In fact, the entire film is set up in Dubai, providing an occasion to show the spaces of a "world city" more glamorous than Bombay.

Ek Haseenah Thi is the tale of a young single Bombay professional woman, Sarika (played by Urmilla Matgaonkar) who is seduced away from her very middle-class values of all-around thrift and caution – both sexual and economic – by a gangster posing as a successful, globe-trotting businessman. The gangster, Karan (played by Saif Ali Khan), frames her in one of his underworld dealings that results in a seven-year prison sentence for her. Sarika is transformed in prison – under the guidance of a woman gangster she learns to fight back and overcome her fears and escapes prison to wreak her revenge on Karan. Sarika sets a trap for him that parallels his cunning framing of her. He ends up on the run from the underworld – that now suspects him of two murders and theft – and the police. Thus, Sarika succeeds in cutting the very grounds of his support out from under him just as he had torn her asunder from her moorings in family and profession. She takes him, in the end, as a prisoner in a prison of her own making – a remote cave with a single torch that soon burns out, leaving him to be eaten alive by rats.

The film opens by establishing Sarika as somewhat stolid, old-fashioned and very rooted in the middle-class mores of sexual modesty and thrift, bound up with maintaining her established boundaries of place and time. She follows her routines as a matter of virtue rejecting spontaneity or exploration – a characteristic that sets her as the opposite of Karan and becomes the basis of her attraction to him. For instance, Karan asks her out to dinner the very first time he meets her at her travel agency when he stops by to pick up his tickets. Sarika refuses to mix romance and work even though her colleague tells her that she would have surely taken the offer if it had come her way. At home, she lives by routines – cleaning her nails, cooking, and cleaning windows, carefully establishing her sexual propriety against popular impressions of the more "liberated" behavior of professional women. For instance, she successfully wards off the unwanted advances of her neighbor and asks Karan to leave when, on his very first visit to her place, he asks her for a kiss. Each action, for Sarika, has a time and place and cannot be rushed.

Karan gradually lures her out of this restraint, seducing her with the thrill of spontaneity, inviting her to live extravagantly and hedonistically in the moment. In a crucial scene that marks the turning point in their relationship, he takes her out to dinner and presents her with an expensive necklace. She demurs and he rebukes her for her outdated beliefs. Arguing that she'd have accepted a pen or flowers as gifts in place of this expensive necklace, he tells her that the necklace was no different from any of those things because he could easily afford it. Articulating the, live-as-if-there-is-no-tomorrow, short-term time-consciousness of capital, Karan convinces Sarika that if you have the money, you live well – you spend it! She takes the necklace and thus starts her initiation into the culture of high spending and high living. In another sequence he invites her to accompany him on a foreign trip for a weekend. "Life is short," he tells her "and comes with no guarantees." He echoes the dictum of the American Express advertisement that in order to save the present from its constant disappearance, one must live in a frenzy of consumption – why settle for the ordinary when you can have something special instead? However much this rush to live in the moment appears to, on the surface, be a bid to forget death, it is in fact a reassertion of its hold on life.

From the way Karan presents himself and speaks of his work, Sarika imagines him to be a member of the new transnational-business or executive class, one of the poster boys of neoliberalism and a highly desired bachelor of contemporary India. Karan dresses and acts like a well-educated, sophisticated member of these elite. His parents, he tells her, are divorced with each living on a different continent – the mother in Europe and the father in the US. In what must be the film's most tongue-in-cheek comment, conscious or otherwise, on the affinity of capital to swindling and cheating, the upwardly mobile transnational executive or businessman is shown to be remarkably similar to a sophisticated gangster.

Andre Gunder Frank (1991) characterized the Latin American economy in the '70s as "Lumpendevelopment," that is, the consequence of a bourgeois economic policy that furthered the dependency of the Latin American economy on global capital along with exacerbating class polarization at home. The gated communities in India mimic the private enclaves that appeared in Latin America following the neoliberal structural "reforms" that were violently enacted there through militaristic coups and with the collaboration of the local elites.

Moreover, the gated community phenomenon is now truly international as affluent islands seek to escape the neighboring ghetto – a fantasy whose US version was recently enacted in *I Am Legend* (Protosevich 2007). While most of the film is preoccupied with images of complete destruction – barely disguised Third World hungry hoards, cast here as virally infected skeletal night beings, feed on flesh and blood in the American urban landscape – the happy ending takes you to a heavy iron gate behind which lies a tree-lined American suburb safe from the invasion of these marauding mobs.

Andre Gunder Frank characterized Lumpendevelopment as a process that could produce a culture of consumption only for a miniscule minority while enhancing the poverty of the many. Rather than invest in public infrastructure at home, dependent economies in Latin America – the home of the first experiments in neoliberalism – were geared towards global capital reinforcing their status as providers of cheap labor and raw materials. Enabling this shift were the so-called "national" elites – the dictators, bureaucrats and intelligentsia who engineered, managed, and justified the military coups under which Latin America was turned toward the free market. "The very same productive forces and structure which promote underdevelopment," Frank concluded, also "produce the high incomes of the Latin American bourgeoisie" (119). This formed the basis of a culture of ostentation and display – a fundamental selfishness.

The lumpen, that is, the dregs or shreds of discarded cloth, as Marx ([1848–50] 2003, 38) used the term, referred to both those on the lowest rungs of the proletariat who could not be employed to produce surplus value and to those sections of the elite who "get rich not by production, but by pocketing the already available wealth of others." Marx offered the following description of the rule of Louis Phillipe, also known as the "banker's king."

> Since the finance aristocracy made the laws, was at the head of the administration of the state, had command of all the organized public authorities, dominated public opinion through the actual state of affairs and through the press, the same prostitution, the same shameless cheating, the same mania to get rich was repeated in every sphere, from the court to the Café Borgne [cafes of dubious reputation] to get rich not by production, but by pocketing the already available wealth of others, clashing every moment with the bourgeois laws themselves, an unbridled assertion of unhealthy and dissolute appetites manifested itself, particularly at the top of bourgeois society – lusts wherein wealth derived from gambling naturally seeks its satisfaction, where pleasure becomes crapuleux [debauched], where money, filth, and blood commingle. The finance aristocracy, in its mode of acquisition as well as in its pleasures, is nothing but the *rebirth of the lumpen proletariat on the heights of bourgeois society*. (38; emphasis original)

This description of the corruptions of the Bonaparte state is remarkably evocative of the corruptions of contemporary India – the stories of kickbacks, bribes, parallel regimes run by paramilitary militias, gangs and finagling that gets reported and forgotten with relentless regularity. The radicalization of finance capital in the twenty-first century has meant, as David Harvey (2005) and David McNally (2009) explain so well, a multiplied risk as finance capital attempts to grow, not through building infrastructure, but through an over-reliance on borrowing and lending, building in an army of brokers who rely on wheeling and dealing. Karan represents the entrepreneurial, lying smooth-talker who makes money out of nothing and merges that attitude in every avenue of his life, including romantic relations. By the end of the film, Sarika too has learned that lesson. So well, in fact, that she beats him at his own game.

Karan tells Sarika that he works in money, making deals here and there, and initiates a mind game by which her own sense of judgment about what is real or not starts to fade. He gets her to sleep with him by playing a game in which she ends up saying "yes" when she means to say "no." Twice, he rescues Sarika from assaults and then later tells her they were set up by him. There is an implicit staging here of a clash between two cultures, between a moral relativism – an aggressive go-getting behavior both at work and in one's personal relations – and an older subjectivity – grounded in middle-class values of saving, hoarding, restraint and caution, an ethic of survival and competitiveness at all costs versus abiding by rules and delayed gratification.

In prison, Sarika is stripped both of middle-class privilege and its accompanying values. Beginning with her inquisitions, which include verbal and physical torture, she is stripped of her sense of personal identity. Checked for lice upon admittance into prison, she learns to sit in line with others and wait for food and finds herself at the mercy of the bullies in prison and in the company of women obviously not of her class. When her parents come to meet her in prison, the camera dwells on their bewilderment as they join a crowd on the other side of the screen to talk with their daughter above the din. Her parents epitomize the salaried middle class – the father is a retired civil engineer and the mother a homemaker. When her father protests to the police that his daughter does not lie, the policewoman retorts cynically:

> How much did you earn? 9,000 Rupees. Your daughter earns 12,000. On top of it, you need these days mobile phones, lipsticks, nail-polishes. […] No father knows what shop his daughter has set up. My daughter does not lie […] huh?

In prison, Sarika slowly learns that her class offers her no protection. Trusting Karan's lawyer that the judge would let her go based on her middle-class affiliations – her education, family and profession – she takes Karan's blame on herself in a bid to protect him from indictment. Instead, the judge imposes the harshest possible sentence based precisely on her class background. It is then that she gives up on seeking justice from the judiciary and adopts the survivalist ethic of the vigilante. Aided by a leading woman gangster who is also in prison, she overcomes her fears and learns to speak the language of the street and wield a knife.

There is a motif – her relationship with rats – that marks Sarika's transformation and the beginning, middle and end of the film. The film opens on a dark image of Sarika watching a rat eat her food in prison and dissolves into a long flashback of her life prior to meeting Karan. We learn that Sarika was mortally afraid of rats. In fact, the very first night she sleeps with Karan – thus stepping outside the parameters the very decorous sexual life she has lived so far – she screamed at the sight of a rat in her kitchen, signifying her vulnerability underneath her independent life. She is, in fact, so terrified of the creature that Karan has to carry her from the kitchen to the bedroom. When the film returns to that opening image in the prison (again towards the middle), she has so changed from her old self that she lifts her plate and, with a carefully calculated aim, deftly kills the rat, thus finally ending the genteel and sheltered phase of her life. At the end of the film, having fully mastered the art of deception and outwitting another, she leaves Karan to rot with rats.

The film, like others in the genre, is very much centered on the anxieties and contradictions of middle-class urban life. Remarking on *Ek Haseenah Thi* as one of a body of films that "offer new modes of engagement with the city [...] an entirely different perceptual entry into the city," Ranjini Mazumdar (2007, 198, 210) suggests that the city emerges here as both a character and space for psychic empowerment. Indeed the film does, as Mazumdar suggests, pull the audience into an unusual spatial experience of the city. We discover the city along with Sarika, traversing its multiple spaces with a speed dictated by an aesthetic of surprise and urgency. Sarika's transformation from a modest middle-class girl into a savvy woman who understands the underworld is shown by the ease with which she begins to straddle the multi-layered, class-divided spaces of the city. The first shots of her life prior to meeting Karan establish the predictable and unchanging routes of her life. She gets off from an auto-rickshaw at her very middle-class high-rise apartment and, warding off the unwanted advances of a neighbor, enters her own domestic space. Her life in the city is confined to her apartment, interspersed with weekends spent with her parents in Pune, a smaller city a few hours away from Bombay.

The Sarika who escapes from the prison has a different relationship to the city altogether. In place of the fixed, convention-bound spaces of her former middle-class life, the city now becomes unhinged from history and acquires the abstraction of a map. First, she goes to a Bombay slum where she meets a gang member who gives her weapons and money. She then follows Karan to Delhi, setting herself up in the Chandini Chowk, an area in the old city, before taking up a room across from Karan's in a fancy hotel. She moves effortlessly through the divided urban landscape of India, taking the slum, the old parts of Delhi and the new shining constructions all in stride and without fear. As she tells Karan when she hands him her death sentence in the cave in a remote part of the abandoned ruins of Tughlaqabad near Delhi, she had found the right place for him only after a great deal of search. Now, Karan is trapped in place, while Sarika is free. The tables have turned.

Sarika's mastery over the city is signaled by the speed and comfort with which she traverses its various segmented parts. Ravi Vasudevan (2004) has described the heightened kinetic engagement and perception of the urban gangster films as an aesthetic effect that enhances the "exhilaration of dread." The gathering sense of anxiety which stalks these films may be attributed to what Moinak Biswas has identified as the "reality effect," that is, the appearance of reality as an aesthetic which draws on television and its obsession with the contemporary (in Vasudevan 2004, 64). Taking this analogy further, one can see that the mixing of documentary and fiction, the appropriation of the aesthetic of immediacy from television and the internet and the collision of spaces in the thriller genre heighten the effect that reality is itself an image, a spectacle.

There is a certain satisfaction of narrative closure offered by cinematic texts that is not available on television. After all, films still have to have – even in this day and age of sequels – a beginning, middle and end. Television, on the other hand, exaggerates the immediacy of the present. Television takes you into the moment, offers its action live and, subsequently, its narratives can do without closure. Live television holds the possibility, Scott McGuire (1998, 253) indicates, of offering a representation that is equal to the "event" showing the radically different or the outside. In cinematic narratives, however, we know that the reality depicted on the screen is produced for us. There is no danger of the world crashing into the fictional space of cinema, despite all of the aesthetics of surprise that cinema may take from documentaries or television. We know that the images on screen are chosen for us and nothing truly unpredictable can occur, unlike in live television (however remote that possibility may be under corporate media, the technology holds that potential). This allows us the reassurance to consume reality as an image, as fiction. As Sarika flies around Delhi and Bombay, the slums and the five-stars all turn into a changing, fluid fiction. The term "reality effect" captures this transformation very well.

It is time, or speed, that effaces places in this film. The city is presented as part of a network united by grids and markers that can be traversed by the tech savvy traveler. The speed with which Sarika criss-crosses this grid extinguishes the distinctions of place and its history, replacing it, instead, with a vivid image of ephemerality. The multiple locations that Sarika moves through produce a new experience of urban space – flyovers, airports, malls, boutiques, discotheques, ATMs and cell phones all collapse distances, subordinating space with time technologies that can enact transfers and exchanges of commodities and information across large distances in the blink of an eye. The editing picks up pace as the film approaches its climax, with spaces collapsing into each other with disorienting speed. For instance, in one scene we see Sarika open a door to follow Karan into a discotheque. The scene cuts to show, in a parallel sequence, the police hot on Sarika's chase breaking into her hotel room. For a split second it appears as if the police have entered the same discotheque door as Sarika. She is, however, one step ahead of them.

The film eschews the aesthetics of direct address – the pattern of repetitions and the epic-inspired, already-known narrative structure of conventional Hindi cinema – in favor of a Hollywood-inspired narrative structure driven by deadlines that aims to suture the spectator with the viewpoint of the protagonist and immerse the spectator into the world of the story. Consequently, suspense is an important desired effect. Sarika's goal is known to the audience and she knows more than Karan. The pleasure is in finding out if she outwits Karan, the underworld and the police to finally get her revenge. The theme song in *Ek Haseenah Thi* does not act as an interruption, but serves as a backtrack that heightens the pulsating tempo of Sarika's transformation. Mazumdar (2007) noted the comfort with which the film shows intimacy between Karan and Sarika, forsaking songs in favor of a direct, subject-centered approach. Moreover, the film eschews the frontal aesthetics of the conventional Hindi film in favor of exploring the cinematic space as three-dimensional, thrusting the viewer into the action in the way of video games (where angles can be manipulated) and the experience of traversing multiple locations on the web.

It visually represents what Paul Virillio ([1991] 2004) called the chrono-politics of contemporary capitalism – a culture of speed characterized by immediacy and instantaneity, creating a subjectivity which is always in a hurry to get somewhere else, to grab at opportunities when they present themselves and to always try to catch up. For these "wired" individuals, places, Virillio tells us, lose their specificity and become points in a network – a subjectivity born of the destruction of urban spaces in post industrial economies of the West at the very moment that other areas were being built up, such as those around large international airports like the Dallas–Fort Worth metroplex. While Virillio made this point in the early '90s, its tendencies have only radicalized as the recovery of postindustrial towns is led by a flashy growth of the so-called "creative economy," that is, turning these former industrial centers into sites of tourism and leisure for an increasingly diminishing elite. There are abandoned homes and ghost towns on one side and glittering shopping venues on the other.

In India, one can see such massive reconstruction in Delhi but Bombay and Kolkata are much too saturated to present drastic vistas of change. The contrasts, however, between places right next to each other is surreal, producing a chrono-politics that is expressed in the common saying that, in India, multiple centuries live alongside. One's dinner in a seven-star hotel may cost more than another's year-long earnings and be assembled with the latest of gadgets and materials from around the world. A stone's throw away, an entire family might be cooking their dinner under a bridge on the street on a make shift stove lit up with wooden sticks. The explanation is not some mystical relationship to time, but the underdevelopment of capitalist development.

Communication technologies have indeed produced a consciousness for which location matters little, distances are collapsed and a radical relativism is produced such that space is to be mastered, not changed. Sarika shows this almost literally – with a map on her windshield and a fast car under her, she follows Karan on highways, keeping tabs on him with her cell phone and managing to stay just a step ahead of him. The middle-class high rise, the Bombay slum, the old city, the *mafiosi* dens, the five-star hotels, all become spots on a grid as does Karan – and ultimately Sarika herself. The subordination of place to abstract space, the reduction of people to targets or marks on a grid and raising speed to an absolute value in itself is the source of a profound moral relativism. In the end, the film does give a nod to the conventional moralistic ending of the Hindi film – Sarika ends behind bars after she has enacted her revenge. Nevertheless, there is a hint of her irrevocable transformation. The last scene shows her looking on at a new prisoner, another lost, middle-class woman like herself who, we are led to believe, Sarika will take under her wing.

The film may be read as a feminist reworking of the conspiracy thriller – its woman protagonist empowered through her knowledge of the utter corruption of the system, a knowledge she passes on to another woman. The question is what kind of feminism is being proposed here? Disassociated from class and the global economy, such role reversal can seem empowering as women take on knowledge previously only accessible to men. In fact, that is the promise of the new culture of consumption targeted at women – it promises women a certain degree of sexual and economic autonomy as consumers. This is embodied in ads for cosmetics and cars, inventing the "new" woman who, according to a celebratory account in *Femina*, a women's lifestyle magazine, is shedding any guilt or embarrassment around personal indulgence to state, "I've made it" (Shridhar 2007). The upwardly mobile woman's comment quoted in this particular issue, "It's my money; I have earned it, so why shouldn't I be demanding? I'm paying for it, so why should I compromise on what I want?" is a class response, no different from the declarations of secession from their Third World neighborhoods made by the gated communities.

The problem is that the freedom of the gated community, the mall or the multiplex is fundamentally unstable, maintained by security and surveillance manned by an urban male proletariat in an increasingly polarizing society. Women have much reason to be afraid, to be paranoid about loss of personal security. One response to this anxiety is the big budget "Bollywood" films obsessed with weddings, the interior décor and domestic rituals of a transnational bourgeoisie that carries its home wherever it goes. In these films, the city of Bombay has disappeared to be replaced by an entirely fictional, generic, "world class" city distinguished as such by global brands and malls.[3]

The other response to the very same sense of dread is the thriller where the city now reappears as a site of danger. The thrills of walking, running and driving through the city offered by these films, I would suggest, appeal to a class and, in particular, to women of that class who are increasingly pushed into a sedentary, static and isolated artificial comfort zone. The speed with which communication technologies collapse distances, multiple screens bring the world within one's grasp, money can be exchanged and objects from the world are brought into the enclosed mall or the gated community is in direct contrast to a body that is restrained and a life lived in fear of others. The virtual experience of the city offered by these films is both a compensation for the absence of and an expression of the fear of real encounters from which the upwardly mobile shield themselves in air-conditioned cars behind tinted glass windows. Is the flight of the protagonist in these films, the urgent race against time, not the understandable psychic response of a subjectivity which must escape the crowd and the ordinary "to arrive," as the ads promise, at a certain coveted address?

CONCLUSION

The beauty and pain of human life stems from our ability to exist between two poles – the actual and the virtual or imaginative. On one end are the constraints, experienced directly and sensuously in both space and time – one's location in place, the mortality of the human body and the social relations of the world we are born into. On the other end is the horizon of freedom opened by the imagination which makes it possible for us to transcend our location in time and space. Yi-Fu Tuan (1977), counter-posing space to place, explains that we live in both the actual and the virtual simultaneously. Place offers us security while space is the site of possibility, of elsewhere. We are attached, Tuan notes, to the former and long for the latter – the former constrains us while the latter may threaten us. In terms of time-consciousness, following Bergson, we understand that humans cannot, like the hands of a clock, be confined to single moments in time that lead mathematically, one into the next. Rather, we defy the pure clock with memory and history, desire and anticipation. Human life is lived in duration and not as "scattered shreds of time" – Marx's characterization of labor under the regime of capital ([1867] 1976, 403).

Freedom then rests, not upon the denial of the integrity of time and space – of what we otherwise call reality, limits or death – but upon our ability to reconcile the imagination with our lived experience, desire with reality. As linguistic beings, we can imagine and build another world and our ability to do so lies in our humanity, our ability to have a language and share a culture. To paraphrase Marx's pithy summation: we make history but not in conditions of our own choosing (Marx [1852] 1999). And the goal is not to increase production or to make it more efficient, but rather to develop humanity itself, to create humans who, Leon Trotsky ([1925] 2005, 207) projected, would be "immeasurably stronger, wiser, and subtler" and whose bodies "more humanized, movements more rhythmic" and voices "more musical." It is, thus, a project that is never completed. And because it requires acting upon and changing reality, it is both realist and revolutionary.

I started this book by indicating that an acute consciousness of time as an antagonist forms the tenor of our times. Time is imagined as an adversary to be raced against until life itself abstracted from time and space appears to be little more than a ticking clock. This is expressed in an acute obsession with youth and novelty – as both appear to ward off death – while in life both the young and the new turn old with increasing rapidity. Moreover, capital has scant regard to spare for the non–profit-generating seasons of human life, such as early childhood and old age when people need care. The entire edifice of commodity culture and incessant labor in capitalism compels us to deny the integrity of our existence in time and space and demands that we, quite literally, sever our connection to our physical bodies and locations and imagine ourselves as no more than measurable units of abstract time.

Such time-orientation runs through the "before" and "after" montages of self-transformation that occur in commodity culture with the regularity of a mantra. We are exhorted to transform ourselves – to become "somebody" who is richer, fairer or sexier – and taught to picture ourselves as images to be doctored and perfected. There is no duration (durée), following Bergson, in the "before" and "after" montage, only discrete moments connected through a linear movement of abstract time. In order to "arrive" ahead of everyone else, the neoliberal subject lives by checklists, sets deadlines, and tears off pages of the calendar with every achievement as if life, itself, were a ticking clock in which the future incessantly dissolves into the present and the present into the past. Time, it appears, is absolute and, like the *Kala* of the *Mahabharata*, holds the universe in its grip. The theme has a particular resonance – as may be observed from the genre that interprets the *Mahabharta* as a manual for living – with the poster-children of neoliberalism, that is, the upwardly mobile professionals making their living in the global corporate machine. After all, the comfort that myth offers is that death is not absolute or final; that the pain of this material life is merely an illusion.

Accommodating oneself to reality in the neoliberal economy entails, Mark Fisher (2009, 54) writes, adapting to a "reality that is infinitely plastic, capable of reconfiguring itself at any moment." From accent schools that teach how to speak in an American accent to a burgeoning gym culture that coaches and goads, self-designing the entire self is now opened for recasting *as-an-image*. For instance, the big weddings I discussed in Chapter 4 are performed with an

Figure 16. An ad for "Fair and Lovely," a skin whitening lotion, presents the lighter faces as a montage, submitting the human to the abstract and homogeneous power of clock time. Positioned as a montage of six faces receding from the whitest in the foreground to the darkest in the background, the ad presents the self as simultaneously fixed and changing. The face remains the same in age – as if no time has passed. Like the disorienting tale of Oscar Wilde's Dorian Gray, whose portrait aged while his face remained youthful as ever, the ad reverses life and image, such that life is turned into an image.

eye to creating future memories, indicating the presumption that the present is already perceived as lost. A new service profession has opened up in this cult of self-presentation and surfaces. Appropriately called image consultants, these professionals offer advice on managing one's persona for social advantage. Along these lines, the brochure of a local gym called Trinity India in the middle-class neighborhood in north Delhi where I live tells its clientele:

> Dancing, health and personality [...] these words are gradually becoming most tempting as well as easily accessible for youth or we would say it is becoming a neccessity or a gateway to success and money. It is pertinent to mention that it is not easy to make a mark in these fields.

Such unremitting demands of constant refasioning produce a profound cynicism regarding the possibility of authentic life and about meaning in general. Parody and irony allow one to conform to the status quo while mocking such conformism. They may also be transformed into resistance against such demands. Nevertheless, such relentless repositioning threatens to empty the self of any coherence. It is best expressed in nihilistic thinking, which, as Stanley Rosen sums up, sees the world, itself, as a "myth in the grip of time" (1999, 48). In essence, nihilism is the expression of a radical historicism that advances the postmodern thesis that we cannot understand the meanings of our own discourses or those of our immediate interlocutors, let alone those of others of another time. The reasoning is that there are no meanings only perspectives or interpretations, and indeed, not even coherent or intrinsically meaningful interpretations, but only continuously changing creations of meaning and value (185).

I have suggested that such nihilist time-consciousness has much in common with the notion of *Maya*, that is, that the world is an image or illusion – an idea that is deeply rooted in Indian aesthetic traditions that have enjoyed a remarkable degree of continuity across history as well as across classical, folk, popular and mass media forms. From a psychoanalytical reading, the denial of reality – which, in essence, is the proposition underlying the notion of *Maya* – may be understood as the response of the human psyche to the trauma of human existence. Unable to conceive of changing the world, one is reassured that its miseries are only temporary and the anguish about death allayed with the assurance that there is a permanence outside of this illusory, mortal life.

That this notion has resonnated for so long, indicates the ongoing anguish of human existence, borne not only out of our incomprehension about death but also compounded by the exceeding cheapening of human life over the course of the last century. The ravages of colonial rule, the forced migration of the Partition and the subsequent decades of underdevelopment have seen the colossal waste of human life and its subordination to the power of wealth. Unable to pay off debts, farmers commit suicide, children slave away their childhoods in backbreaking work, and the goal of life is turned simply into surviving another day. And the notion of *Maya* has been embraced with alacrity by the middle class and the elites. It helps them cope with the uncertainties, the ups and downs of the free market and the absurd demand that the goal of life is not life, but the accumulation of wealth. Moreover, religion serves as a wily glue – it establishes commonality with the dispossessed without necessarily calling for a redistribution of wealth.[2]

A dread of the future douses the culture of capitalism and underlies its nihilistic time-consciousness. The obsession with youth in commodity culture may well be seen as a response to the loss of meaning such subjectivity entails. The predominant images of youth in capitalist culture are not of young people as labor, but overwhelmingly as buyers; and youth itself is offered as the ultimate promise of commodity culture. Thus, capital appears to extend youth and its attributes of freedom, i.e., the possibility of changing the future. Capitalism promises youth to anyone who can buy it. Yet, this is not to be confused with freedom. The expanding uncertainty and risk accompanying capitalist expansion has made life for everyone appear ever more dependent upon accidents of fate and tied the young even more to the fortunes or commands of their elders. Meanwhile, the obsession with profit calculations, which is held higher than life itself, incessantly destroys the present, hurtling us towards an out-of-control future. Life appears to be in the grip of time and at its mercy.

In India's turn to neoliberalism, there may be observed all of the symptoms of the capitalist invasion of time. While as humans we must struggle with the limits and mystery of death, with what it is to be free in both living and dying, capital turns time into an ever-diminishing currency whose value for each individual depends upon her or his place in the market. In the war between capital and labor, the most profitable and efficient situation for capital is one in which labor, shorn of all of all resistance, appears before capital with nothing to sell but time. And, it is in the interests of capital to relentlessly reduce the market value of this time. The fear of falling down the market hierarchy thus haunts everyone.

Hans Jonas (1966), who lost his mother in the Nazi concentration camps and escaped that ending himself, said that nihilism was a response to the end of our belief in immortality. "Our presumptive immortality," Jonas writes, "[…] appears suddenly at the mercy of a moment's miscalculation, failure, or folly by a handful of fallible men. What has dramatically shifted is that we know the mortality of human civilization, that we are perishable. And that which is perishable cannot keep immortality" (266). In other words, we are now fully aware that humanity may, itself, become history.

Poised as antagonists and competitors within capitalism, the only logical way to confront this crisis is to let disaster strike others, to hope, let the flood come after me – *après moi le déluge* – which Marx had identified as the hallmark emotion of capitalism. It is akin to riding a train hurtling along at breakneck speed and hoping it will not crash. Under the regime of capital, the only reward for living with such disregard for the future is the ability to buy market-produced commodities, an array of services and things that can be acquired based upon one's purchasing power. The ideological glue that holds all this together is the myth of choice in the free market. Disavowing the congenital bond between an individual's purchasing power and position in the labor market, capitalist commodity culture attributes magical properties to the commodity, expecting it to create conditions of freedom.

In contrast, socialism – with its attention to transforming the material conditions of our lives – embraces praxis as a way of life worthy of human existence and interjects the human in natural time as well as in history. Praxis is the meeting of the body and the mind, the material and the imaginative, and in acting upon the world we ourselves are transformed. History, for Marx, moves dialectically. As Michael Lowy (1981, 27) puts it, it moves through "innumerable combinations, fusions, discontinuities, ruptures and sudden qualitative leaps." But, the creative element in history – as in production – is human labor, and human labor is inseparable from the imagination. The imagination weaves together time, connecting the past to the future and thus, giving meaning to our actions in the present. Praxis, that is, an ever spiraling effect of action informed by thought and thought informed by action, opens up the present as a space of possibility in which the past and the future may be reconciled. It keeps both time and space intact even against the relentless interruptions of an antagonistic society. Perhaps, the ability to act upon memory and with desire is our real wealth. People struggle to redeem the injustices of the past while hoping for a better future. Yet, for Marx nothing in history was preordained and, in the final analysis, it was human action – that is, class struggle – that moved history, restored the individual to the social, and reconciled the self with itself, others and nature. It is thus we come to occupy time rather than merely submit to its passing.

NOTES

Introduction   After Me the Flood

1 In Rahman 2002, 157

2 I agree with the critical readings of the film's ideological affinity to neoliberalism. For instance, Nandini Chandra (2010b) explains that it casts the affluent middle class exclusively as the voice of political agency raised against a weak state, whose only problem is corruption. Neelam Srivastava (2009) has commented on the film's denial of the Marxist revolutionary politics of Bhagat Singh, turning it instead into a useful tool for the construction of a militaristic Indian national identity – the film presents two alternatives for patriotism, the military or the IAS (Indian Administrative Service). Aarti Wani (2007) has noted that the film works to taming and channeling student discontent towards servicing the neoliberal state rather than destroying it. While these readings of the dominant meanings of the film are correct, they do not fully explain the deep resonance of the film with young, middle-class people or the energy of its appeal in terms such as the RDB generation (*Rang De Basanti* generation) or the film's tagline, "A Generation Awakens." The visceral response the film evoked amongst the young, urban middle class, I believe, has to do with the disillusionment it expresses with the hollowness of consumer culture while holding out the possibility of taking charge of history and setting it correct. In what has to be one of the first in Hindi cinema, it depicts the murder of the father by the son – all in the way of saving the nation from the elders who have forgotten its history. The tragic irony of the film is that the young are awakened to a history the elders have forsaken, but it tempers that irony with hope as, in the act of remembering, the young are reconciled with the past. The energy of the film's music and its juxtapositions of the present and the past are anything but cynical.

3 Press Information Bureau 2007; on inaugurating a three-day congregation of Indian diaspora on Sunday in the capital (New Delhi).

4 "Like the universe as a whole, each conscious being taken separately, the organism which lives is a thing that endures. Its past in its entirety, is prolonged into its present, and abides there, actual and acting" (Bergson 1911a, 15; see also Bergson 1911b, 75–7).

5 I am relying here on Deleuze's ([1966] 1991) account of Henri Bergson's philosophy of time where he distinguishes the actual, which occurs in the realm of experience in the present, from the virtual, which functions at the level of ideas and images as in memory and fantasy.

6 As a working journalist, Marx had personal experience of this. He was contracted by the *Tribune*, based in the US, to write for the paper. The terms were that he was to give them two articles – they would pay him for one, whether they printed it or not. As for the second, they would pay if they used it. Marx wrote to Engels, "In spite of their

very *amicable* tone it is evident that I have understood those gentlemen correctly [...] In essence, they are reducing me to one half. Nevertheless I am *agreeing to it* and *must agree to it*" ([1857] 1980; emphasis original, letter dated 24 March 1857).

7 "[Capital] allows its actual movement to be determined as much and as little by the sight of the coming degradation and final depopulation of the human race, as by the probable fall of the earth into the sun" (Marx [1867] 1976, 381).

8 I have discussed this in relation to the US in *Coining for Capital* (2005). See also Thomas C. Frank (1997), Rob Latham (2002), Gary Cross (1997) and Juliet B. Schor (2004).

9 Thanks to Nandini Chandra for this observation.

10 Thanks to Sue Ferguson, personal correspondence.

11 Khap panchayats are local government bodies in the state of Harayana (on the border of Delhi) that are comprised of the rich farmer lobby that benefitted from the Green Revolution and are now powerful conservative voices. They also have considerable power at the center.

12 For a transcript of this news story, see Indo Asian News Service 2010.

13 Personal notes (23 April 2010).

Chapter 1   Brand India's Biggest Sale: The Cultural Politics and Political Economy of India's "Global Generation"

1 (1867) 1976, 795.

2 In Kripalani 2000.

3 IBEF homepage. Online: http://www.ibef.org/about-us.aspx (accessed 19 August 2013).

4 This is a revised version of a paper presented at the Historical Materialism Conference, Toronto, 2008, in a panel with Sue Ferguson, Beryl Langer and Alan Sears. I AM grateful for their very helpful comments and camaraderie.

5 A similar process may be observed in Japan. Based on an ethnographic study of middle-class Japanese children in the 1990s, Norma Field (1995) concluded that their childhood was being increasingly colonized by the logic of ceaseless production as children are socialized into laboring adults. Anne Allison (1996) offers an insightful and nuanced account of mothers' labor in socializing children in the performance centered disciplinary regime of Japanese pedigree society and the accompanying anxieties around sexuality and intimacy.

6 See Nandini Chandra (2010a) for an account of the continued integration of the disciplined child, tied to the language of merit, into the nation-building project in post-independence Hindi cinema.

7 See Luxton 2006; Brenner and Laslett 1991.

8 See J. Kapur 2005.

9 In a discussion I heard amongst Indian mothers in the US of Amy Chua's (2011) well-known book on the rigors of Asian parenting, a mother reported that she takes a different tact from Chua's slave driving. The mother always travels first-class to India, impressing upon her children that if they do not work hard in school they would have to travel in economy with the masses!

10 I frequently heard older women complain about younger women's expenditures on children's clothes and toys and the younger women responded that these expenditures have to be done, "there is no choice."

11 For examples, see Arjun Appadurai (1990) and Homi Bhabha (1994).

12 From an advertisement for Lodha Fiorenza, "signature duplex sky villas."

13 See Jeremy Seabrook (2001) and Viviana Zelizar (1985) for an excellent summary of the arguments nineteenth-century capitalists made in support of child labor.

14 J. Kapur (2005) and S. Ferguson (2009) make the point that adult anxieties around consumer culture stem, in fact, from our awareness that children's commodity culture brings children into a relationship with capitalism only too well known to the adult.

Chapter 2   Arrested Development and the Making of a Neoliberal State

1 Literally translating to "mother-father," the term refers to a conception of the state and the ruling elites as benevolent patriarchs who take care of their subjects.

2 I will develop this further in Chapter 3 which explicitly deals with time consciousness.

3 Perry Anderson, "After Nehru," *London Review of Books* 34, no. 15 (2 August 2012): 21–36.

4 Randhir Singh would often challenge students with the Socratic question: "Define democracy?" Well-schooled in our civics lessons, we would respond that it was government of the people, for the people and by the people. "Then, why are the people poor?" would be the quick rejoinder.

5 I remember my friend, Vrinda Grover – who must have been eighteen or nineteen at that time – sarcastically remarking that we would all get there anyway. It was not, as she elaborated, that the twenty-first century was a place we could not step into without Rajiv Gandhi's help. Ironically, we did get there without him.

6 The *Mahabharata* is one of India's two oldest epics, dated back to somewhere around 400 BCE, it is nevertheless alive in cultural forms. I relied upon Rajagopalachari's 2005 edition.

7 Yoga literally means unity or oneness of body and mind and being with the universe. It involves the erasure of boundaries around the self, including the weight of the body or flesh and a sense of individuation, including memory and relationships that tie the self to concrete, material life. For psychoanalytical insights (a study that begins with the premise of the individual) into what this entails for the individual read Sudhir Kakkar's novel, *Ecstasy* (2001).

8 Why US business schools have such a significant number of Indians is yet to be explored, but their presence has certainly eased the transition to neoliberalism as Indian governments, since the '80s, have relied on their expertise in policy and as go-between between Indian and global capital.

9 Dale Carnegie's *How to Win Friends and Influence People* (1937), which advised that financial success depended overwhelmingly on people skills, is considered the grandfather of this genre.

10 The postmodern counterpart of this lesson in the advanced capitalist countries is, as Slavoj Žižek (2002) describes the statement, "I did it because I did it." Or one can add: "I did it but I did it ironically, with a savvy acknowledgement of its meta-discourse" (137).

11 *Kahaani* literally means "story."

12 Described in more detail in Chapter 3.

13 For a very clear and well-supported discussion on the roots of Schopenhauer's thought in the concept of *Maya*, see Douglas Berger (2004).

14 From a personal conversation with Satish Bhatia, filmmaker and film teacher at Xavior's Institute of Communications (XIC), Mumbai who was explaining why he could not take up a nine-to-five job.

15 Vidya Chhabria, who successfully took over the reins of the $2 billion Jumbo Group after her husband Manu Chhabria's death in 2002, and Naina Lal Kidwai, the highest paid woman executive in the country, are the two Indians picked by *Fortune* magazine in its 50 Most Powerful Women in Business.

Chapter 3   For Some Dreams a Lifetime is Not Enough: The *Rasa* Aesthetic and the Everyday in Neoliberalism

1 *Paise vasool ho gaye*, that is, "It was well worth my money," is a common way to show appreciation for a film packed with several attractions. A short film is seen as cheating the cinema-goer of such pleasures.

2 Holi is a spring festival associated with the erotic legends around Krishna.

3 Vasudevan makes this compelling argument, supporting it with a fine and nuanced reading of a song from *Pyaasa* (Guru Dutt 1957) (Vasudevan n.d.).

4 The male proletariat is now segregated in the cheaper, older, single movie theaters and other proletarian venues, such as tent theaters in small towns and rural areas or video parlors in city slums. Earlier, such stratification was enforced within the space of the single theater, with the front benches reserved for working-class men and the more expensive balconies above for "ladies" and "families." The song and dance sequences or item numbers provided a carnivalesque opportunity for the front benchers to flaunt a sexualized masculinity in the face of the respectable balcony-seaters. The aggression against all women and the invisibility of working-class women implicit in such display must undercut any celebration of this as a straight-forward enactment of class conflict.

5 A number of factors have, since the 1990s, enabled a shift in Hindi cinema towards strengthening an authorial vision as well as plots that emphasize individual psyches. Filmmakers are now able to raise money from banks and recover costs by exhibiting to niche audiences in multiplexes, thus making it possible to bring new narratives and themes to the screen.

6 For an account of the work of producing these soaps, see Shoma Munshi (2010).

7 For my generation, born in the '60s, this is still a striking shift from state-owned television and its three hours of daily operation in the '70s. Since the '80s, television hours have consistently increased.

8 *Chawls* are one-room tenements in multi-storied building with shared toilets and bathrooms. These were traditionally the residences of the Bombay industrial working class and known for their close knit communities.

9 From the 19 September 2012 episode.

10 For *Rasa* in Indian performance, see Richard Schechner (2001), Anuradha Kapur (1990) and Philip Lutgendorff (2006).

11 See Akhil Gupta (1992), Dipesh Chakrabarty (1997) and Bliss Cua Lim (2009) for an argument about alternative temporalities.

12 Nehru had established the Indian Institute of Management, Calcutta and Ahmadabad in 1962. Initially used for working executives, the institutes turned into highly prestigious educational institutions for acquiring an MBA. When I joined college in 1980, we had

just heard of this degree and it was beginning to overtake Civil Service as the most sought-after middle-class career choice. It also represented a shift away from the liberal arts education demanded of the colonial bureaucracy towards an emphasis on the workings of the market and a pragmatic indifference to theory or history. MBAs then turned out to be typically highly paid but overworked individuals whose experience of culture was yuppified – or limited to opportunities for consumption as a way to assert class distinction. The privatization unleashed in the '80s brought with it the valorization of the MBA as a sought-after degree for the nation's brightest graduates.

13 A spate of books on winding alumni careers may be found in the market. See Rashmi Bansal's *Stay Hungry Stay Foolish* (2008), the title borrowed from Steve Jobs' address to the Stanford University class of 2005.

14 For examples see Shaifali Sandhya (2009) and Ashok K. Banker (2012).

Chapter 4   An "Arranged Love" Marriage: India's Neoliberal Turn and the Bollywood Wedding Culture Industry

1 It is not that opulent weddings are new to Bombay cinema or the hyper visible lives of its star members, what is new about these contemporary weddings, I hope to show, is a reinvention of tradition enacted as choice and a marker of identity.

2 Dowry was one of the main issues in the women's movement of the '80s. Campaigns against dowry included street theater, oaths taken by young women to refuse dowry, social boycott of families known to take dowry and systematic surveys which established the link between the death of young women in their marital homes and domestic abuse related to dowry. These efforts led to the passing of a law which requires the immediate arrest and investigation of all the members of the woman's marital home if she is brought to a hospital with burns or other fatal forms of injury.

3 Chakravarty 1993, 55, cited in Hirji 2005.

4 *Indian Express* 2007a; in a speech delivered to the Confederation of Indian Industry 23 May 2007, New Delhi.

5 A lakh is equivalent to the number 100,000.

Chapter 5   *Ek Haseenah Thi* (There Once Was a Maiden): The Vanishing Middle Class and Other Neoliberal Thrills

1 Reality & Verticals 2010; real estate advertisement for housing in Nirvana Country, Gurgaon.

2 Rather than dismiss paranoia as an irrational state, Jameson locates it in specific historical conditions.

3 For more elaboration, see Jyotsna Kapur and Manjunth Pendakur (2007).

Conclusion

1 1999, 181.

2 See Ananya Mukherjee-Reed (1997) for an analysis of how the Hindu Right reconciles private ownership with populism.

REFERENCES

Audiovisual Sources

Ahmed, Shiraz, Jitendra Parmar and Anurag Prapanna. 2007. *Naqaab*, directed by Abbas Burmawalla and Mastan Burmawalla. Nimbus Motion Pictures, India. DVD, 115 min.

Balani, Anant (dir.). 2003. *Ek Din 24 Ghante*. Channel Nine Entertainment Ltd., India. DVD, 95 min.

Barjatya, Sooraj (dir.). 1994. *Hum Aapke Hain Kaun…!* Rajshri Productions.

Barjatya, Sooraj R., Kamal K. Bartajya and Ravindra Jain. 2006. *Vivah: A Journey From Engagement to Marriage*. Ultra DVD Video, Mumbai. DVD.

Bazmee, Anees, Rumi Jaffery and Rajan Agarwal. 2004. *Mujh Se Shaadi Karogi*. Nadiadwala Grandson Entertainment Pvt. Ltd. Film.

Desai, Shamin. 2012. *Rush*, directed by Shamin Desai and Priyanka Desai. Percept Pictures.

Gadhvi, Sanjay and Mayur Puri. 2002. *Mere Yaar Ki Shaddi Hain*, directed by Sanjay Gadhvi. Yash Raj Films.

Gupta, Raj Kumart (dir.). 2008. *Aamir*. UTV Motion Pictures.

Iyengar, Niranjan. 2003. *Kal Ho Naa Ho*, directed by Nikhil Advani. Yash Raj Films International, Wembley, UK.

Johar, Karan (dir.). 1998. *Kuch Kuch Hota Hai*. Dharma Productions.

Johar, Karan and Sheena Parikh. 2001. *Kabhi Khushi Kabhi Gham*, directed by Karan Johar. Yash Raj Films, Mumbai.

Joshi, R. M. et al. 2007. *Teen Bahuraniya*, directed by Swapna Joshi, Pawan Kumar, Nandita Mehra and Bhagwan Yadav. Television series premiered 26 March, ended 9 January 2009. Playtime Creationn, India.

Joshi, R. M. and Shirish Latkar. 2010. *Pavitra Rishta*, directed by Sameer Kulkarni and Bhavin Thakkar. Television series premiered 1 June, ongoing. Balaji Telefilms, Mumbai. Online: http://apni.tv/serials/pavitra-rishta.html (accessed 2 June 2010).

Kapoor, Ekta. 2007. *Ekta Kapoor Talk Asia Show*, CNN, 29 March.

Khan, Farah, Mayur Puri and Mushtaq Sheikh. 2007. *Om Shanti Om*, directed by Farah Khan. Eros Entertainment.

Khan, Tanveer and Dilip Shukla. 2006. *Deadline: Sirf 24 Ghante*, directed by Tanveer Khan. Percept Picture Company.

Mehra, Rakyesh Omprakash and Renzil D'Silva. 2006. *Rang De Basanti*, directed by Rakyesh Omprakash Mehra. UTV Motion Pictures.

Moore, Michael (dir.). (1989) 2003. *Roger & Me*. Warner Home Video, Burbank, CA.

Palekar, Amol (dir.). 2005. *Paheli*. Red Chilies Entertainments, Mumbai.

Pandey, Neeraj (dir.). 2013. *A Wednesday!* Premiered 15 July. UTV Motion Pictures.

Protosevich, Mark et al. 2007. *I Am Legend*, directed by Francis Lawrence. Warner Bros. Pictures. DVD, 100 min.

Raghavan, Sriram and Pooja Ladha Surti. 2004. *Ek Haseenah Thi*, directed by Sriram Raghavan. DVD, 137 min.

Textual Sources

Ahmed, Aijaz. 1992. *In Theory: Classes, Nations, Literatures*. London: Verso.

_____. 1995. "The Politics of Literary Postcoloniality." *Race & Class* 36: 1–21.

Alanen, Leena. 1994. "Gender and Generation: Feminism and the 'Child Question'." In *Childhood Matters: Social Theory, Practices and Politics*, edited by Jens Ovortup, Marjatta Bardy, Giovanni Sgritta and Helmut Wintersberger, 27–42. Aldershot: Avebury.

Allison, Anne. 1996. *Permitted and Prohibited Desires: Mothers, Comics and Censorship in Japan*. Boulder, CO: Westview Press.

Amin, Samir. 2005. "India: A Great Power?"*Monthly Review* 56, no. 9 (February). Online: http://monthlyreview.org/2005/02/01/india-a-great-power (accessed 12 July 2013).

Anderson, Perry. "After Nehru." *London Review of Books* 34, no. 15 (2 August 2012): 21–36.

Appadurai, Arjun. 1990. "Disjuncture and Difference in the Global Cultural Economy." *Theory, Culture & Society* 7: 295–310.

ApunKaChoice Bureau. 2004. "Rohit Bal to Launch Kid's Designer Line Bal Bachche." ApunKaChoice.com, 26 October. Online: www.apunkachoice.com/scoop/fashion/20041026-0.html.

Arendt, Hannah. 1968. *Imperialism: Part Two of the Origins of Totalitarianism*. New York: Harcourt Brace Janovich.

Bagchi, Amiya. 2006. "Neoliberal Imperialism, Corporate Feudalism and the Contemporary Origins of Dirty Money." Networkideas.org. Online: http://www.networkideas.org/feathm/may2006/Amiya_Bagchi.pdf (accessed 20 August 2010).

Bajoria, Jayashree. 2004. "Disney Launches India TV Channels." BBC News, 17 December. Online: http://news.bbc.co.uk/2/hi/south_asia/4104089.stm (accessed 12 July 2013).

Banerjee, Soumyadipta. 2013. "Shah Ruskh Khan Charges a Hefty Amount for Weddings." *Mumbai Mirror*, 11 May.

Banerjee, Subhajit. 2006. "Date with Disneyland." *Telegraph*, 22 January. Online: http://www.telegraphindia.com/1060122/asp/calcutta/story_5752681.asp (accessed 24 June 2007).

Banker, Ashok K. 2012. *The Valmiki Syndrome: Finding the Work-Life Balance*. Noida: Random House.

Bansal, Rasmi. 2008. *Stay Hungry Stay Foolish*. Ahmedabad: CIIE.

Basu, Dipankar and Pratyush Chandra. 2007. "Neoliberalism and Private Accumulation in India." *Radical Notes*. 7 February. Online: http://radicalnotes.com/content/view/32/30/ (accessed 18 March 2011).

BBC News. 2005. "Coke Told to Close Indian Plant." BBC News, 19 August. Online: http://news.bbc.co.uk/2/hi/business/4167606.stm (accessed 13 July 2013).

Berardi, Franco. 2011. *After the Future*, edited by Gary Genosko and Nicholas Thoburn. Edinburgh, Oakland, Baltimore: AK Press.

Berger, Douglas. 2004. *"The Veil of Maya": Shopenhauer's System and Early Indian Thought*. Binghampton: Global Academic Publishing.

Bergson, Henri. 1911a. *Creative Evolution*, translated by Arthur Mitchell. New York: Henry Holt.

_____. 1911b. *Matter and Memory*, translated by Nancy Margaret Paul and W. Scott Palmer. London: George Allen and Unwin.

Bhabha, Homi. 1990. *Nation and Narration*. London: Routledge.

_____.1994. *The Location of Culture*. New York: Routledge.

Bhagwati, Jagdish. 2004. *In Defense of Globalization*. New York: Oxford University Press.

Bharucha, Rustom. 1995. "Utopia in Bollywood: 'Hum Aapke Hai Kaun...!'" *Economic and Political Weekly* 30, no. 15: 801–4.

Bhupta, Mallini. 2001. "Mind over Mattel." *Economic Times*, 3–9 August: 4.

Borges, Jorge Luis. 1999. *Selected Poems*, edited by Alexander Coleman. New York: Penguin Books.

Bourdieu, Pierre. 1984. *Distinction: A Social Critique of the Judgement of Social Taste*, translated by Richard Nice. London: Routledge & Kegan Paul.

_____. 1993. *Sociology in Question*, translated by Richard Nice. New Delhi: Sage.

Brecht, Bertolt. (1933–47) 1957. *Brecht on Theater: The Development of an Aesthetic*, edited by John Willet. New York: Hill and Wang.

Brenner, Johanna and Barbara Laslett. 1991. "Gender, Social Reproduction and Women's Self-Organization: Considering the U.S. Welfare State." *Gender and Society* 5, no. 3: 311–33.

Brooks, Peter. 1976. *The Melodramatic Imagination*. New York: Columbia University Press.

Brown, Wendy. 2003. "Neo-liberalism and the End of Liberal Democracy." *Theory and Event* 7, no. 1. *Muse*. Online: http://muse.jhu.edu/journals/theory_and_event/summary/v007/7.1brown.html (accessed 12 July 2013).

Carnegie, Dale. (1937) 1998. *How to Win Friends and Influence People*. New York: Pocket Books.

Chakrabarty, Dipesh. 1997. "The Time of History and the Times of the Gods," in *The Politics of Culture*, edited by Lisa Lowe and David Lloyd, 35–60. Durham, NC: Duke University Press.

Chakravarty, Sumita. 1993. *National Identity in Indian Popular Cinema, 1947–1987*. New Delhi: Oxford University Press.

Chandra, Nandini. 2010a. "Merit and Opportunity in the Child-Centric Nationalist Films of the 1950s," in *Narratives of Indian Cinema*, edited by Manju Jain, 123–44. New Delhi: Primus.

_____. 2010b. "Young Protest: The Idea of Merit in Popular Hindi Cinema." *Comparative Studies of South Asia, Africa and the Middle East* 30, no. 1 (May): 119–32.

Chatterjee, Debashis. 2012. *Timeless Leadership: 18 Leadership Sutras from the Bhagavad Gita*. Singapore: Johnn Wiley and Sons.

Chodorow, Nancy. 1978. *The Reproduction of Mothering: Psychoanalysis and the Sociology of Gender*. Berkeley: University of California Press.

Chua, Amy. 2011. *The Battle Hymn of the Tiger Mom*. London: Penguin Books.

Clark, Brett, John Bellamy Foster and Richard York. 2009. "Capitalism in Wonderland." *Monthly Review* 60, no. 1 (May): 1–18.

Coles, Robert. 1986. *The Moral Life of Children*. Boston: Houghton Mifflin Company.

Cross, Gary. 1997. *Kids' Stuff: Toys and the Changing World of American Childhood*. Cambridge, MA: Harvard University Press.

Das, A. 2005. "Middle-Class India Plows New Wealth into Big Weddings." *Christian Science Monitor*, 9 September. Online: http://www.csmonitor.com/2005/0929/p01s04-wosc.html (accessed 12 July 2013).

Das, Gurcharan. 2001. *India Unbound: A Personal Account of a Social and Economic Revolution from Independence to the Global Information Age*. New York: Alfred Knopf.

_____. 2009. *The Difficulty of Being Good: On the Subtle Art of Dharma*. Delhi: Penguin Books.

David, Ruth. 2007. "India Responds To Allegations of Child Labor for Gap." *Forbes*. Online: http://www.forbes.com/2007/10/31/gap-subcontracting-india-markets-equity-cx_rd_1031markets01.html (accessed 12 July 2013).

Deleuze, Gilles. 1986. *Cinema 1: The Movement Image*, translated by Hugh Tomlinson and Barabara Habberjam. London: Athlone.

_____. 1989. *Cinema 2: The Time-Image*, translated by Hugh Tomlinson and Robert Galeta. London: Athlone.

_____. (1966) 1991. *Bergsonism*, translated by Hugh Tomlinson and Barbara Habberjam. New York: Zone.

Desai, Kiran. 1999. *The Inheritance of Loss*. New York: Grove Press.

Devi, Mahasweta. (1978) 1993. "Shishu," in *Women Writing in India, Volume II: The 20th Century*, by Susie Tharu and K. Lalita, 236–51. New York: The Feminist Press.

Eagleton, Terry. 1981. *Walter Benjamin or towards a Revolutionary Criticism*. London: Verso.

_____. 2007. *The Meaning of Life: A Very Short Introduction*. New York: Oxford University Press.

Edmunds, June and Bryan S. Turner. 2005. "Global Generations: Social Change in the Twentieth Century." *British Journal of Sociology* 56, no. 4: 559–77.

Ehrenreich, Barbara. 1990. *Fear of Falling: The Inner Life of the Middle Class*. New York: Harper Perennial.

Elsaesser, Thomas. 1987. "Tales of Sound and Fury," in *Home Is Where the Heart Is: Studies in Melodrama and the Women's Film*, edited by Christine Gledhill, 43–69. London: BFI.

Engels, Frederick. (1891) 2000. "Introduction to Karl Marx's Wage Labor and Capital." *Marxist/Engels Internet Archive*. Online: http://www.marxists.org/archive/marx/works/1847/wage-labour/intro.htm (accessed 15 July 2013).

Engels, Fredriech and Karl Marx. (1848) 2005. *The Communist Manifesto: A Road Map to History's most Important Political Document*, edited by Phil Gasper. Chicago: Haymarket Books.

Economic Times Bureau. 2009. "Raju Was Riding a Toothless Tiger." *Economic Times*. 14 April. Online: http://articles.economictimes.indiatimes.com/2009-04-14/news/28435498_1_satyam-founder-b-ramalinga-raju-satyam-shares (accessed 13 July 2013).

Ferguson, Sue. 2009. "Toys, Capitalism and Commodification: Fantasy or Myth." Unpublished paper presented at the conference Historical Materialism at York University in Toronto, Canada, 24–6 April 2008. Modified 2009 in personal correspondence.

Fernandes, Leela. 2000. "Nationalizing the Global: Media Images, Cultural Politics and the Middle Class in India." *Media, Culture and Society* 22, no. 5: 611–28.

_____. 2006. *India's New Middle Class: Democratic Politics in an Era of Economic Reform*. Minneapolis: University of Minnesota Press.

Field, Norma. 1995. "The Child as Laborer and Consumer: The Disappearance of Childhood in Contemporary Japan," in *Children and the Politics of Culture*, edited by Sharon Stephens, 51–78. New Jersey: Princeton University Press.

Fischer, Karin. 2010. "In India, a Student-Recruiting Industry Ups the Ante for U.S. Colleges." *Chronicle of Higher Education*, 10 January.

Fisher, Mark. 2009. *Capitalist Realism: Is There No Alternative?* Winchester: O Books.

Frank, Andre Gunder. 1991. "The Underdevelopment of Development." Online: http://www.druckversion.studien-von-zeitfragen.net/The%20Underdevelopment%20of%20Development.htm (accessed 2 April 2011).

Frank, Thomas C. 1997. *The Conquest of Cool: Business Culture, Counterculture, and the Rise of Hip Consumerism*. Chicago: University of Chicago Press.

Friedman, Thomas. 2005. *The World is Flat: A Brief History of the Twenty-First Century*. New York: Farrar, Straus and Giroux.

Gahlaut, Kanika. 2007. "Nobody Can Make or Break You but Yourself." *Indian Express*, 3 March. Online: http://www.indianexpress.com/news/nobody-can-make-or-break-you-but-yourself/24754/0?q=&stype=indianexpress&srch=&city=delhi&mod=dsearch. (accessed 12 July 2013).

Ghosh, Jayati and C. P. Chandrashekhar. 2002. *The Market that Failed: A Decade of Neoliberal Economic Reforms in India*. New Delhi: Leftword.

Ghosh, Sujoy. 2012. *Kahaani: A Mother of a Story*, directed by Sujoy Ghosh. Performed by Vidya Balan. Boundscript.

Gilbert, David. 2006. *Stumbling upon Happiness*. New York: Vintage.

Giroux, Henry. 2009. *Youth in a Suspect Society: Democracy or Disposability?* New York: Palgrave.

Gopalan, Lalitha. 2002. *Cinema of Interuptions: Action Genres in Contemporary Indian Cinema*. London: BFI.

Gupta, Akhil. 1992. "The Reincarnation of Souls and the Rebirth of Commodities: Representations of Time in 'East' and 'West'." *Cultural Critique*, no. 22 (Autumn): 187–211.

Harvey, David. 2005. *A Short History of Neoliberalism*. Oxford: Oxford University Press.

_____. 2010. *The Enigma of Capital and the Crises of Capitalism*. London: Profile Books.

Hengst, Heinz. 2005. "Complex Interconnections: The Global and the Local in Children's Minds and Everyday Worlds," in *Studies in Modern Childhood: Society, Agency, Culture*, edited by Jens Qvortrup, 21–38. New York: Palgrave.

Hindu Business Line Bureau. 2005. "Disney Characters to Perform Life." *Hindu Business Line*, 29 December. Online: http://www.thehindubusinessline.com/todays-paper/tp-marketing/disney-characters-to-perform-live/article2199864.ece (accessed 12 July 2013).

Hirji, Faiza. 2005. "When Local Meets Lucre: Commerce, Culture, and Imperialism in Bombay Cinema." *Global Media Journal* 4, no. 7. Online: http://lass.purduecal.edu/cca/gmj/fa05/graduatefa05/gmj-fa05gradref-hirji.htm (accessed 12 July 2012).

Horkheimer, Max and Theodore Adorno. (1972) 1993. "The Culture Industry: Enlightenment as Mass Deception," in *Enlightenment as Mass Deception*, translated by John Cumming, 29–43. London: Routledge.

Huws, Ursula. 2003. *The Making of a Cyberatariat*. New York: Monthly Review Press.

Indian Express. 2007a. "Manmohanomics II: Thou Shall Not Flaunt Thy Wealth and Greed." *Indian Express*, North American edition, 1 June: 5. Online: http://www.indianexpress.com/news/manmohanomics-ii-thou-shall-not-flaunt-thy-wealth-and-greed----------------/31819/ (accessed 12 July 2013).

_____. 2007b. "At 7, Sushma Becomes Youngest Matriculate." *Indian Express*, North American edition, 7 June: 7. Online: http://www.indianexpress.com/news/at-7-sushma-becomes-youngest-matriculate/32819/ (accessed 12 July 2013).

_____. 2009. "Buckle up, Indians Are Coming: Obama to Americans." *Indian Express*, 12 June. Online: http://www.indianexpress.com/news/buckle-up-indians-are-coming-obama-to-americans/475324/ (accessed 10 April, 2011).

Indiantelevision.com Team. 2005. "KidZee Opens Five More Pre-school Centers at Bangalore." Indian Television, 27 June. Online: www.indiantelevision.com/mam/headlines/y2k5/june/junemam137.htm (accessed 12 July 2013).

Indo Asian News Service. 2010. "School Kids Made to Walk on Embers, Glass in Gujarat." India-Forums, 21 April. Online: http://www.india-forums.com/news/national/243226-school-kids-made-to-walk-on-embers-glass-in-gujarat.htm (accessed 19 July 2013).

Jameson, Fredric. 1992. "Totality as Conspiracy," in *The Geopolitical Aesthetic: Cinema and Space in the World System*, 9–84. Bloomington: Indiana Univeristy Press and BFI.

_____. 1998. "Cognitive Mapping" in *Marxism and the Interpretation of Culture*, edited by Cary Nelson and Lawrence Grossberg, 347–57. Urbana: University of Illinois.

Jonas, Hans. 1966. *The Phenomenon of Life: Toward a Philosophical Biology*. New York: Harper and Row.

Kabir, Nasreen. 1999. *Talking Films: Conversations on Hindi Cinema with Javed Akhtar*. New Delhi: Oxford University Press.

Kakkar, Katharina and Sudhir Kakkar. 2007. *The Indians: Portrait of a People*. Delhi: Penguin Books.

Kakkar, Sudhir. 1978. *The Inner World: A Psychoanalytic Study of Childhood and Society in India*. Delhi: Oxford University Press.

_____. 2001. *Ecstasy*. Delhi: Penguin Books.

Kapur, Anuradha. 1990. *Actors, Pilgrims, Kings and Gods: The Ramlila at Ramnagar*. Kolkata: Seagull Books.

Kapur, Jyotsna. 1998. "It's a Small World After All: Globalization and Transformation of Childhood in India." *Visual Anthropology* 11: 387–97.

_____. 2005. *Coining for Capital: Movies, Marketing, and the Transformation of Childhood*. New Jersey: Rutgers University Press.

_____. 2007. "Ghosts of Christmas Past, Rising from the Gaps of Capital." *Monthly Review Zine*. 24 December. Online: http://mrzine.monthlyreview.org/2007/kapur241207.html (accessed 2 April 2011).

Kapur, Jyotsna and Manjunath Pendakur. 2007. "The Strange Disappearance of Bombay from its Own Cinema: A Case of Imperialism or Globalization." *Democratic Communique* 22, no. 1: 43–59.

Kaushik, Narendra. 2005. "NASA Boy Turns Out to Be Fraud." *Asian Tribune*, 1 March. Online: http://www.asiantribune.com/news/2005/03/01/nasa-boy-turns-out-be-fraud (accessed 12 July 2013).

Klawans, Stuart. 2007. "The Things They Carried." *Nation*, March. Online: http://www.thenation.com/article/things-they-carried-0?page=0,1 (accessed 12 July 2012).

Kraidy, Marwan. 1999. "The Global, the Local, and the Hybrid: A Native Ethnography of Glocalization." *Critical Studies in Mass Communciation* 16: 457–76.

Kripalani, Manjeet. 2006. "Selling India Inc. at Davos." *Business Week*, January. Online: www.businessweek.com/bwdaily/dnflash/jan2006/nf20060130_4381_db032.htm (accessed 2011).

Kroll, Luisa and Kerry A. Dolan. 2013. "The World's Billionaires." *Forbes*, 3 April. Online: http://www.forbes.com/billionaires/ (accessed 12 July 2013).

Kurtz, Stanley. 1992. *All the Mothers Are One: Hindu India and the Cultural Reshaping of Psychoanalysis*. New York: Columbia University Press.

Landa, Ishay. 2007. *The Overman in the Marketplace: Nietzchean Heroism in Popular Culture*. New York: Lexington Books.

Langer, Beryl. 2004. "The Business of Branded Enchantment: Ambivalence and Disjuncture in the Global Children's Culture Industry." *Journal of Consumer Culture* 4, no. 2: 251–77.

_____. 2011. "Children, Consumption, and the Logic of Capitalism." Unpublished paper presented at the conference Historical Materialism at York Univerisity,

Toronto, Canada, 24–6 April 2008. Modified 2009 in personal correspondence; updated 2011.

Latham, Rob. 2002. *Consuming Youth: Vampires, Cyborgs, and the Culture of Consumption*. Chicago: University of Chicago Press.

Lefebvre, Henri. 1987. "Everyday and Everydayness." *Yale French Studies* 73: 7–11.

_____. 1995. *Introduction to Modernity*, translated by John Morore. London: Verso.

Lim, Bliss Cua. 2009. *Translating Time: Cinema, the Fantastic, and Temporal Critique*. Durham, NC: Duke University Press.

Lowy, Michael. 1981. *The Politics of Combined and Uneven Development: The Theory of Permanent Revolution*. London: Verso.

Lukose, Rittu. 2009. *Liberalization's Children: Gender, Youth, and Consumer Citizenship in Globalizing India*. Durham, NC: Duke University Press.

Lutgendorf, Philip. 2006. "Is There an Indian Way of Filmmaking?" *International Journal of Hindu Studies* 10, no. 3 (December): 227–56.

Luxton, Meg. 2006. "Feminist Political Economy and Social Reproduction," in *Social Reproduction: Feminist Political Economy Challenges Neo-liberalism*, edited by Kate Bezanson and Meg Luxton, 11–44. Montreal: McGill-Queen's University Press.

Mannheim, Karl. 1997. "The Problem of Generations," in *Collected Works of Karl Mannheim*, vol. 5, 276–320. London: Routledge.

Marx, Karl. 1843. "Letter to Ruge, Dresden." *Marxist Internet Archive*. Online: http://www.marxists.org/archive/marx/works/1843/letters/43_09-alt.htm (accessed 12 July 2013).

_____. (1845–46) 1978. *The German Ideology*, edited by Robert C. Tucker. New York: Norton.

_____. (1850) 2003. *The Class Struggles in France, 1848–1850*. With an introduction by Doug Lorimer. Chippendale, Australia: Resistance Books.

_____. (1852) 1999. "Chapter 1," in *The Eighteenth Brumaire of Louis Bonaparte*, translated by Saul K. Padover. *Marx/Engels Internet Archive*. Online: http://www.marxists.org/archive/marx/works/1852/18th-brumaire/ (accessed 13 July 2013).

_____. (1857) 1980. "Personal Letter to Engels, March 24, 1857," in *Karl Marx – Friedrich Engels: Selected Letters, Personal Correspondance 1844–1877*, edited by Fritz J. Raddatz, 93. Boston: Little, Brown and Company.

_____. (1867) 1976. *Capital Vol. 1*. London: Penguin Books.

Mascarenhas, Anuradha. 2004. "Teen IT Whizkid is Nation's Toast." *Indian Express*, North Atlantic edition, 26 November.

Mazzarella, William. 2003. *Shovelling Smoke: Advertising and Globalization in Contemporary India*. Durham, NC: Duke University Press.

Mazumdar, Ranjini. 2007. *Bombay Cinema: An Archive of the City*. Minneapolis: Minnesota University Press.

McGuire, Scott. 1998. *Visions of Modernity: Representation, Memory, Time and Space in the Age of the Camera*. New Delhi: Sage Publications.

McNally, David. 2001. *Bodies of Meaning: Studies on Language, Labor, and Liberation*. Albany: State University of New York Press.

_____. 2009. "From Financial Crisis to World Slump: Accumulation, Financialization, and the Global Slowdown." *Historical Materialism* 17, no. 2: 35–83.

Meehan, Eileen. 1993. "Commodity Audience, Actual Audience: The Blindspot Debate," in *Illuminating the Blindspots: Essays Honoring Dallas W. Smythe*, edited by Vincent Mosco, Manjunath Pendakur and Janet Wasko, 378–400. Norwood, NJ: Ablex.

Mehra, Rakyesh Omprakash and Renzil D'Silva. 2006. *Rang De Basanti*, directed by Rakyesh Omprakash Mehra. UTV Motion Pictures.

Menon, Nivedita. 2012. "Feminism and the Family – Thoughts on International Women's Day." *Kafila*, 8 March. Online: http://kafila.org/2012/03/08/feminism-and-the-family-thoughts-on-international-womens-day/ (accessed 12 July 2013).

Metz, Christian. 1977. *The Imaginary Signifier: Psychoanalysis and the Cinema*. Bloomington: Indiana University Press.

Modleski, Tania. 1984. "The Rhythms of Reception: Daytime Television and Women's Work," in *Regarding Television: Critical Approaches – An Anthology*, edited by Ann E. Kaplan, 67–74. Frederick, MD: University Publications of America.

Mukherjee-Reed, Ananya. 1997. "The State as Charade: Political Mobilisation in Today's India." *Socialist Register* 33: 245–64.

Munshi, Shoma. 2010. *Prime Time Soap Operas on Indian Television*. Delhi: Routledge.

Nair, Priya and K. Ram Kumar. 2009. "Banks Aim to Score Big with Education Loans." *Hindu Business Line*, 15 November.

Nandy, Ashis. 1983. *The Intimate Enemy: Loss and Recovery of Self under Colonialism*. New Delhi: Oxford University Press.

_____. 1995. *The Savage Freud and Other Essays on Possible and Retrievable Selves*. Princeton: Princeton University Press.

Narayan, Ramesh. 2005. "Brand India Revisited." Hindu Business Line. 3 March. Online: www.thehindubusinessline.com/bline/catalyst/2005/03/03/stories/2005030300240400.htm (accessed 6 April 2006).

Nayar, Sheila. 1996. "National Identity in Indian Popular Cinema, 1947–1987." *Journal of Popular Culture* 31, no. 1: 73–90.

Nirali Magazine. 2007. "Filming Your Shaadi Story." NiraliMagazine.com, 7 June. Online: http://niralimagazine.com/2007/06/filming-your-shaadi-story/ (accessed 12 July 2013).

Osborne, Peter. 1995. *The Politics of Time: Modernity and the Avant Garde*. London: Verso.

Pendakur, Manjunath. 2003. *Indian Popular Cinema; Industry, Ideology and Consciousness*. New Jersey: Hampton Press.

Perry, Celia. 2007. "Woe Christmas Tree: Wal-Mart Buys Ornaments from a Chinese Sweatshop." *Mother Jones*. 14 December. Online: http://www.motherjones.com/politics/2007/12/woe-christmas-tree-wal-mart-buys-ornaments-chinese-sweatshop (accessed 18 July 2012).

Picchio, Antonella. 1992. *Social Reproduction: The Political Economy of the Labor Market*. Cambridge: Cambridge University Press.

Pinney, Christopher. 2008. *The Coming of Photography in India*. London: British Library.

Porter, Michael. 1990. *The Competitive Advantage of Nations*. New York: Free Press.

Prahalad, C. K. 2006. *The Fortune at the Bottom of the Pyramid*. Upper Saddle River, NJ: Pearson Education, Inc.

Prasad, Madhava. 1998. *Ideology of the Hindi Film: A Historical Construction*. New Delhi: Oxford University Press.

Press Information Bureau. 2007. "PM's Address at Pravasi Bharatiya Diwas." Press Information Bureau, Government of India, 7 January. Online: http://pib.nic.in/newsite/erelease.aspx?relid=23847 (accessed 10 July 2013).

Purie, Aroon. 2006. "Hype and Hardsell – Davos 2006: India Showcases Contemporary Face at World Economic Forum." *India Today*, 13 February. Online: http://indiatoday.

intoday.in/story/davos-2006-india-showcases-contemporary-face-at-world-economic-forum/1/181922.html (accessed 13 July 2013).

Radhakrishna, G. S. 2005. "Moral Police Prowl Hyderabad Parks." *Telegraph*, 11 April. Online: http://www.telegraphindia.com/1050411/asp/nation/story_4600371.asp (accessed 12 July 2013).

Rahman, Sarvat. 2002. *100 Poems by Faiz Ahmed Faiz*. New Delhi: Abhinav Publications.

Rai, Saritha. 2004. "Indian Venture Reincarnates Spider-Man." *International Herald Tribune*, 22 November.

Rajadhyaksha, Ashish. 2003. "The 'Bollywoodization' of the Indian Cinema: Cultural Nationalism in a Global Arena." *Inter-Asia Cultural Studies* 4, no. 1: 25–39.

Rajagopalachari, C. 2005. *Mahabharata*. Mumbai, Maharashtra: Bharatiya Vidya Bhavan.

Rajalakshmi, T. J. 2008. "No Mechanism to Protect the Poor: Interview with Utsa Patnaik." *Frontline*, 12–25 April. Online: http://www.hinduonnet.com/fline/fl2508/stories/20080425250802400.htm (accessed 17 March 2011).

Ramesh, Jairam. 2005. "Defining Brand India." *Hindu Business Line*. Online: http://www.thehindubusinessline.in/bline/catalyst/2005/02/24/stories/2005022400020300.htm (accessed 12 July 2013).

Ramesh, Randeep. 2006. "A Tale of Two Indias." *Guardian*, 5 April. Online: http://www.guardian.co.uk/world/2006/apr/05/india.randeepramesh2 (accessed 12 July 2013).

Ramoji Film City. n.d. "Weddings." RamojiFilmCity.com. Online: http://www.ramojifilmcity.com/tourist/weddings-coverage.html (accessed 12 July 2013).

Reality & Verticals. 2010. Advertisement. RealityVerticals.com. Online: http://realtyverticals.com/projects.php?meid=60&act=&proj_id=22 (accessed 12 July 2013).

Rodricks, W. 2007. "Fashion Forward." *Femina*, 17 January: 86–8.

Rosen, Stanley. 1969. *Nihilism: A Philosophical Essay*. New Haven: Yale University Press.

———. 1999. *Metaphysics in Ordinary Language New Haven and London 1999*. New Haven, London: Yale University Press.

Saamna. 2005. "'If a Man Is Provoked by Such Clothes, Who Can One Blame?'" OutlookIndia.com, 25 April. Online: http://www.outlookindia.com/article.aspx?227237 (accessed 12 July 2013).

Sabarinath, M. and Krishna Gopalan. 2009. "India Inc Waits with Its Finger on the Trigger." *Economic Times*, 23 November.

Sainath, P. 2009. "HDI Oscars: Slumdogs versus Millionaires." *India Together*, 19 March. Online: http://www.indiatogether.org/2009/mar/psa-forbes.htm (accessed 12 July 2013).

Sandhya, Shaifali. 2009. *Love Will Follow: Why the Indian Marriage Is Burning*. Noida: Random House.

Sarkar, Sumit. 1997. *Writing Social History*. New Delhi: Oxford University Press.

Sarkar, Tanika. 2001. *Hindu Wife, Hindu Nation: Community, Religion and Cultural Nationalism*. New Delhi: Permanent Black.

Schechner, Richard. 2001. "Rasaesthetics." *Drama Review* 45, no. 3: 27–50.

Schor, Juliet B. 2004. *Born to Buy: The Commercialized Child and the New Consumer Culture*. New York: Scribner.

Seabrook, Jeremy. 2001. *Children of Other Worlds: Exploitation in the Global Market*. London: Pluto Press.

Shivshankar, Shobita. 2012. "It's Shoe Time." *Tribune*, 14 July: 2–3.

Singh, Randhir. 1993. "In Memory of Punjab Revolutionaries of 1914–1915," in *Five Lectures in Marxist Mode*, 91–121. Delhi: Aakar Press.

_____.1999. "Of Nationalism in India: Yesterday, Today and Tomorrow." *Mainstream* (August): 27–36.

_____. 2006. *Crisis of Socialism: Notes in Defense of a Commitment.* Delhi and London: Ajanta Books.

_____. 2010. "MARX SERIES No. 11: A Note on the Current Political Situation and a Conclusion." *Mainstream* 48, no. 34 (August).

Shridhar, Pruabi. 2007. "Ah, Affluence." *Femina*, 17 January: 146.

Smith, Zadie. 2000. *White Teeth.* London: Penguin Books.

Soto, Hernando de. 1989. *The Other Path: The Economic Answer to Terrorism.* New York: Harper and Row.

Srivastava, Amit. 2004. "Coca-Cola Spins Out of Control in India." India Resource Center, 15 November. Online: http://www.indiaresource.org/campaigns/coke/2004/cokespins.html (accessed 2 April 2011).

Srivastava, Neelam. 2009. "Bollywood as National(ist) Cinema: Violence, Patriotism and the National-Popular in *Rang De Basanti*." *Third Text* 23, no. 5 (November): 703–16.

Sutton-Smith, Brian. 1986. *Toys as Culture.* London: Gardner Press.

Swift, Jonathan. 1729. "A Modest Proposal: For Preventing the Children of Poor People in Ireland from Being a Burden to Their Parents or Country, and for Making Them Beneficial to the Public." *The Artbin Origo.* Online: http://art-bin.com/art/omodest.html (accessed 16 March 2011).

Tabb, William. 2007. "Imperialism: In Tribute to Harry Magdoff." *Monthly Review* 58, no. 10: 26–37.

Tharoor, Shashi. 2007. "A Billion Indias Now." *Indian Express*, North American edition. 5 June: 6.

Thompson, E. P. 1967. "Time, Work-Discipline and Industrial Capitalism." *Past and Present* 38 (December): 56–97.

TNN. 2003. "Indian Women Find Favour with Fortune." *Times of India*, 7 October. Online: http://articles.timesofindia.indiatimes.com/2003-10-07/india/27173524_1_indian-women-naina-lal-kidwai-manu-chhabria (accessed 13 July 2013).

Trotsky, Leon. (1925) 2005. *Literature and Revolution.* Chicago: Haymarket Books.

Tuan, Yi-Fu. 1977. *Space and Place: The Perspective of Experience.* Minneapolis: University of Minnesota Press.

Tudor, Deborah. 2011. "Twenty-First Century Neoliberal Man," in *Neoliberalism and Global Cinema: Capital, Culture and Marxist Critique*, edited by Jyotsna Kapur and Keith Wagner, 59–78. New York: Routledge.

Uberoi, Patricia. 2006. *Freedom and Destiny: Gender, Family, and Popular Culture in India.* New Delhi: Oxford University Press.

United States Department of Labor. 2012. Web pages under titles "Employment" and "Unemployment." Bureau of Labor Statistics. August. Online: http://www.bls.gov/cps/ (accessed 30 September 2012).

Varma, Pawan K. 1999. *The Great Indian Middle Class.* New Delhi: Penguin Books.

Vasudevan, Ravi. 1995. "Addressing the Spectator of a 'Third World' National Cinema: The Bombay of Social Film of the 1940s and 1950s." *Screen* 36, no. 4: 305–24.

_____. 2000. "The Politics of Cultural Address in a 'Transitional' Cinema: A Case Study of Indian Popular Cinema," in *Reinventing Film Studies*, edited by Christine Gledhill and Linda Williams, 130–64. London: Arnold.

_____. 2004. "The Exhilaration of Dread: Genre, Narrative Form and Film Style in Contemporary Urban Action Film." *Sarai Reader 02: The Cities of Everyday Life*, 59–67. Delhi: Sarai.

_____. 2011. *The Melodramatic Public: Film Form and Spectatorship in Indian Cinema.* New York: Palgrave Macmillan.

Vinayak, Achin. 2004. "The Politics of Neoliberalism in India," interview by Ganesh Lal. *International Socialist Review* (January–February): 54–9.

Virillio, Paul. (1991) 2004. "The Overexposed City," in *The Paul Virillio Reader*, edited by Steve Redhead, 83–100. New York: Columbia University Press.

Vrinda, Sharma. 2010. "Khap Panchayat' Leaders Condemn Court Ruling." *Hindu*, 14 April. Online: http://www.hindu.com/2010/04/14/stories/2010041461720100.htm (accessed 10 July 2013).

Wani, Aarti. 2007. "Uses of History: Rang de Basanti and Lage Raho Munnabhai." *Monthly Review Zine*, 12 February. Online: http://mrzine.monthlyreview.org/wani120207.html (accessed 20 August 2013).

Weil, Robert. 2008. "City of Youth: Shenzhen, China." *Monthly Review* 60, no. 2 (June): 32–49.

Wilkie, Rob. 2002. "How 'New' is the New Labor and (Some Notes on) Its Relation with Cyberculture." *Red Critique*, July–August. Online: www.redcritique.org/july-august02 (accessed June 2012).

Zelizar, Viviana A. 1985. *Pricing the Priceless Child: The Changing Social Value of Children.* New York: Basic Books.

Žižek, Slavoj. 2002. *Welcome to the Desert of the Real.* London: Verso.

INDEX